Groundfighting Pins
and Breakdowns

Effective Pins and Breakdowns for Judo, Jujitsu, Submission Grappling and Mixed Martial Arts

Groundfighting Pins and Breakdowns

*Effective Pins and Breakdowns for Judo, Jujitsu, Submission
Grappling and Mixed Martial Arts*

By Steve Scott

    Turtle Press   Santa Fe

To contact the author or to order additional copies of this book:
call 1-800-778-8785 or visit www.TurtlePress.com

ISBN 978-1-934903-03-5
LCCN 2008006893
Printed in the United States of America

10 9 8 7 6 5 4 3 2 1 0

Warning-Disclaimer

This book is designed to provide information on specific skills used in judo, jujitsu, sambo, grappling and other martial arts. It is not the purpose of this book to reprint all the information that is otherwise available to the author, publisher, printer or distributors, but instead to compliment, amplify and supplement other texts. You are urged to read all available material, learn as much as you wish about the subjects covered in this book and tailor the information to your individual needs. Anyone practicing the skills presented in this book should be physically capable to do so and have the permission of a licensed physician before participating in this activity or any physical activity.

Every effort has been made to make this book as complete and accurate as possible. However, there may be mistakes, both typographical and in content. Therefore, this text should be used only as a general guide and not the ultimate source of information on the subjects presented here in this book on sambo or any skill or subject. The purpose of this book is to provide information and entertain. The author, publisher, printer and distributors shall neither have liability nor responsibility to any person or entity with respect to loss or damages caused, or alleged to have been caused, directly or indirectly, by the information contained in this book.

Library of Congress Cataloguing in Publication Data

Scott, Steve, 1952-
  Groundfighting pins and breakdown : effective pins and breakdowns for judo, jujitsu, submission grappling and mixed martial arts / by Steve Scott.
      p. cm.
  ISBN 978-1-934903-03-2
  1. Martial arts--Holding. 2. Hand-to-hand fighting. I. Title.
  GV1102.7.H64S37 2008
  796.815--dc22
                                    2008006893

Acknowledgements

Thanks to the following people for appearing in the photos used in this book: John Saylor, Shawn Watson, Bryan Potter, Chris Heckadon, Bob Rittman, Drew Hills, Bill West, Trevor Finch, Eric Millsap, Mark Lozano, Josh Henges, John Zabel, John Begley, Kyle Meredith, Jake Phillips, Nick Rothwell, Erik Butler, Kirt Yoder, Mike Copeland, Jon Taylor, Kirk Quinones, Alan Johnson, Ben Goehrung, Jarrod Fobes, Kelly Hunter, Vince Vitatoe, Chance Powers, Bret Holder, Ed Rogers, Travis Oliphant, Greg Fetters, Mike Thomas, Andy Fonseca, Ronnie Oswald, Bill Henninger, Steve Palma, Chris Garlick, Chas Owen and Josh Crawford. Photos were taken at Welcome Mat, the Barn of Truth and Bill Brown's Karate. Steve Scott, Mark Lozano, Jorge Garcia, Brett Holder, Bill Brown, Ed Rogers, Andy Fonseca, Eric Millsap and Jamie Scott took photos for this book.

Contents

INTRODUCTION

Pins, hold-downs and the skills that put an opponent in these predicaments, breakdowns, are some of my favorite aspects of grappling. I often tell the athletes who train with me that pins and hold-downs are like loyal friends. They're there when you need them.

Hold-downs and pins are the workhorse techniques of any type of grappling, whether it is judo, jujitsu, sambo, submission grappling or any form of wrestling. To some people, they are the least glamorous of all grappling skills. Basically, you hold your opponent down on the mat or ground and don't let him up. Nothing spectacular, unless you're the guy on top who just won the match! Maybe you didn't force your opponent to tap out or submit from an armlock, choke or leglock, but you still beat him and proved dominance over him. Holding someone down and not letting him up isn't a fluke. It takes effort and it takes skill. Like anything else, techniques in judo, sambo, jujitsu, self-defense and submission grappling are subject to what's stylish or the latest trend. When a great champion or fighter uses a particular move, everyone seems to want to copy it or at least learn it. Trends in techniques, like trends in fashion or in any phase of life, come and go. Pins and hold-downs seem to be the moves that are always there, even when other moves are considered "cool" or in style, they're the moves that you can rely on when you need to beat an opponent. They're like that old friend; there when you need them. Over the many years Welcome Mat has been in existence, we have spent many hours on the mat working on what takes up many pages of this book, with a particular interest in breaking down an opponent from a stable to an unstable position, no matter what the starting position may be. The athletes and coaches who have worked with me over the years have taken a particular interest in this phase of groundfighting. While no claims are made for the originality of any techniques presented in this book, Welcome Mat athletes have tested and refined them in thousands of judo, sambo, sport jujitsu and grappling matches in many parts of the world.

This book is for anyone who participates in any form of grappling, sport combat, martial arts or self-defense. My background is in judo, sambo and Shingitai Jujitsu but I am a keen admirer of the legitimate professional wrestlers who flourished in America in the early part of the 20th century. The skills, tactics and ideas in this book have a lot of carry-over value to any grappling activity, so if you're a judoka looking for some more information on how to excel at your sport, you'll get as much out of this book as the submission grappler or mixed martial arts fighter who's looking for realistic and effective skills to help him win. I believe a good pin is the end result of you breaking your opponent down and putting him in a vulnerable position.

For your reference, this book isn't divided into sections based on particular pins. Rather, the emphasis will be on how to get your opponent into a pin and then hold him there. While there are a good number of effective pins, there are even many more ways of breaking your opponent down and putting him into a position so that you can apply a pin.

Many thanks go to all the members of the Welcome Mat Judo, Jujitsu and Sambo Club for their help in making this book possible. As with all of my books, the photographs used were taken during workouts on the mats at the Welcome Mat gyms and dojos. I am fortunate to have many talented athletes, coaches and students who train with me and their ideas and support made this book all the better. Many thanks go to Mark Lozano for taking a good number of the photos in this book. Mark is a professional photographer, a black belt in judo and a valued coach at Welcome Mat. I would also like to thank Turtle Press and Cynthia Kim for their support and technical help. My dear friend John Saylor, Director of the Shingitai Jujitsu Association, helped a great deal on ideas on the content of this book. As always, my wife Becky (the first American woman to win a World Sambo Championship in 1983) was a great help in editing and offering advice on how to make this book better. My goal has been to produce a book that you can refer to time and again for many years and use as a reliable source of information. If this book has helped you achieve a better understanding of groundfighting, pins and hold-downs, or if you use anything you've learned from this book to pin an opponent in practice or competition, then my goal as a coach and author has been fulfilled.

This book is dedicated to my dear friend, Bob Corwin, one of the finest men and one of the best coaches I have had the pleasure of knowing and working with. I value Bob's friendship and wisdom. He is one of the most technically sound and innovative coaches to ever step on a mat. His "bread and butter" approach to coaching at his Yorkville, Illinois judo club has produced hundreds of national and international judo and sambo champions, but his moral and ethical integrity make him the great man he is.

Steve Scott

Grappling From An Historical Perpective

The pins and breakdowns presented in this book all have a common root. That root is Kodokan Judo and the various jujitsu and grappling systems that contributed to the early development of judo. That root has grown and branched off in many directions and this is reflected on these pages as well and I want to give credit where credit is due. There have been many influences on grappling and combat sports since Professor Jigoro Kano founded Kodokan Judo in 1882. It was Prof. Kano and his revolutionary approach to the theory and technique of the Japanese fighting disciplines that were commonly called jujutsu that established the premise and set the course we have taken. But, the history and evolution of grappling is a long, varied and rich one with contributions from many people, cultures and approaches to throwing, holding and manipulating the human body. Almost every culture on earth has some kind of grappling, wrestling or fighting sport or art native to that culture.

Because of the mingling of people and cultures due to the ease of ability to travel in the 20th century, people have learned fighting arts and sports from one place, modified them to suit the needs and interests of their own culture or way of doing things and developed hybrid martial sports. Sports (and fighting arts) like sambo from the former Soviet Union, legitimate professional wrestling from the early 20th century in America, the style of grappling that came to be known as Brazilian jiujitsu from Brazil, Greco-Roman wrestling from France, Shooto and Pancrase from Japan and mixed martial arts (MMA) from America, plus many other forms of hybrid grappling and fighting have contributed to the body of knowledge that exists today. Basically, an effective hold or technique is effective no matter what you call it or who taught it to you.

The Japanese approach to holding an opponent to the mat is called "osae waza (or osaekomi waza)" or immobilization or restraining techniques. The word osae means, "to restrain" or "immobilize" and osaekomi means "to put into a restraint" or "to apply an immobilization" technique. Osae waza is different than the western concept of wrestling where you pin your opponent's shoulders to the mat to show dominance and achieve victory. In the western tradition of wrestling, or as in legitimate professional wrestling of past years, pinning your opponent's shoulders to the mat simultaneously for up to 3 seconds won the match. In the Japanese approach to grappling and wrestling that was heavily influenced by the sport of judo in the late 1800s

11

and early 1900s, restraining your opponent for an extended period of time on the ground or mat with the intention of applying a submission technique is considered showing dominance. You don't have to pin your opponent's shoulders to the mat to beat him. Instead, your goal is to keep him under control with him mostly on his back or backside. However, this wasn't always the case. In the many jujutsu (also spelled jujitsu or jiujitsu) systems of feudal Japan, the osae waza (restraining or immobilization techniques) emphasized having your opponent face down on the ground rather than face up as is now the custom in sport judo and other grappling styles. The reason that the old jujitsu systems emphasized pinning an opponent face down on the ground was for purely martial and self-defense reasons. In the same way a police officer today gets an assailant to the ground to control him and apply the handcuffs, the feudal jujitsu masters developed immobilization techniques to dominate their opponents. Jujitsu wasn't a competitive activity or sport. It was first and foremost a fighting art and the Japanese jujutsu exponents used osae waza to restrain an opponent long enough to apply a joint lock, choke, striking technique or even use some type of weapon to inflict further damage and finish him off. With this historical perspective of immobilizing an opponent so that a submission technique (or worse) could be applied, when judo developed as a method of sport combat, it embraced the idea of holding an opponent to the mat, as we now understand it.

As grappling and martial sports of other cultures evolved in the 20th century (as mentioned earlier) the concept of osae waza (even though the Japanese name was not retained or even considered in some cases) became the primary approach to holding an opponent to the mat. The men who developed sambo and Brazilian jiujitsu initially studied judo and made it the basis for their particular approaches to grappling.

Although wrestling and grappling sports have existed for thousands of years in almost every culture, grappling began to come into its own during the late 1800s through early 1900s in many parts of the world. From our American perspective, the rough and tumble professional wrestlers of the early 20th century who barnstormed across the United States did much for the development of wrestling. These legitimate professional grapplers used the European method of showing dominance with a pin by achieving victory when both an opponent's shoulders were held to the mat for 3 seconds (and not the Japanese approach to pinning). The wide variety of technically sound grappling and wrestling moves these athletes used was astonishing. Men like Farmer Burns, Frank Gotch, Ed "Strangler" Lewis and many others developed professional wrestling in America to a legitimate, and unique, grappling sport. Legitimate professional wrestling may have died out, but the technical skills these grappling masters left us survive.

Newaza (groundfighting) from the Japanese perspective, developed to a high technical level by the exponents of Kosen Judo in pre-World War II Japan. The Kosen Judo movement was organized at a number of Japanese universities and emphasized the groundfighting of Kodokan Judo over the throwing techniques. After the war, only a few universities continued Kosen Judo, but its influence on Japanese judo was profound. Another period of technical development in groundfighting came after Anton Geesink of Holland won the gold medal in the 1964 Olympics in the Open category in judo, defeating the Japanese Akio Kaminaga with a pin. The Japanese were shocked (to say the least) that Geesink won the gold medal in the premier event (the Open category) in the very first Olympic Games where judo was staged (in the sport they invented). The importance of groundfighting, and pinning an opponent in particular, had been hammered home. It's my belief that Geesink's use of groundfighting to win the Olympics led to a worldwide appreciation of its importance.

The internationalization of judo opened the floodgates of technical development in all aspects of grappling. Sambo athletes in the Soviet Union had been honing their skills in relative obscurity but when they burst onto the international judo and wrestling scene in the 1960s, they brought with them some of the most innovative groundfighting skills yet seen on international mats. Judo was introduced to the Soviet Union in the early 1900s by Vasili Oshchepkov and he and his colleagues wasted no time in blending many of the native styles of grappling such as Kuruash from central Russia, Gulesch from Azerbaijan, Chida-Oba from Georgia and other folk styles from other parts of the Soviet empire with judo. This blending of judo with native folk wrestling eventually came to be known as sambo in the late 1930s. The Soviets looked at international sporting events as another avenue for proving their political system was superior to others and when they took to the world stage in the 1960s in both judo and wrestling, the Soviet Union's athletes and coaches held nothing back in their quest for gold medals in all styles of mat sport combat. Whether it was judo, wrestling or their native sambo, the Soviets certainly believed that function dictated form and they pushed the limits of technical development in all phases of grappling, wrestling and sport combat. Their innovative approach opened the door to many new hybrid grappling styles and the effect the sambo wrestlers had on international judo was profound.

As the European judo athletes and coaches learned more about the sambo approach to grappling, they incorporated it into their judo and challenged the dominance of the Japanese. The period of 1962 to 1992 saw a major change in how judo (in general) and groundfighting (in particular) was thought of, taught and practiced. This was a period of great technical growth for groundfighting and the sport of judo in general. The early 1990s saw Brazilian jiujitsu increase in popularity, especially in the United States. The Brazilians have approached groundfighting from their perspective and have laid major importance to fighting from their backsides from (what they named) the guard position. The Brazilian trend revived and updated newaza as practiced in the early days of Kodokan Judo. In an approach similar to Kosen Judo, the Brazilian jiujitsu movement has done much for the development of groundfighting in the late 20th century and early 21st century.

The advent of mixed martial arts in the 1990s has led to another level of development in the history of grappling and sport combat. It is more than obvious that to be a well-rounded fighter and succeed in the rough and tumble sport of mixed martial arts, you have to know how to grapple on the ground. It's my belief that the backbone of the sport of mixed martial arts is grappling. Sure, punches and kicks are important in this sport (and in self-defense in general) and I certainly don't discount their effectiveness, but like my old coach Jerry Swett used to tell us; "If you're not afraid to go to the mat, you'll be more confident in your standing attacks." However, to be a complete grappler or fighter, you must have a good standing game; it's essential. Any grappler who fails to be well rounded or neglects any phase of fighting will certainly have flaws. A grappler may be able to hide his flaws against inferior opposition, but when he steps up in competition, flaws will turn into weaknesses and good opponents will take advantage of it. While Olympic and collegiate wrestling continue to use the concept of pinning an opponent's shoulders to the mat as a method of beating him, many modern styles of grappling and combat sports have adopted judo's approach to holding an opponent to the ground and this approach is reflected in this book.

What To Expect From This Book

Along with the holding techniques shown in this book, my primary goal is to show how breaking an opponent down and putting him in the position to secure the hold or pin is essential to being a skillful groundfighter. Your opponent isn't going to lie down for you and let you pin him. You have to do something to get him into that pin and the best way to do it is to break him down. I believe an effective pin is the end result of an effective breakdown. Some call these moves "turnovers" and while that name may be acceptable, I prefer to call these skills "breakdowns." A breakdown implies an aggressive act and dominance over your opponent. It also describes what you are doing; you are breaking him down from a stable to an unstable position. You may not always turn him over but you are always breaking him down so you can put him in a position to pin or hold him. Many breakdowns take place when both grapplers are on hands and knees or lying on the mat, but a number of breakdowns presented in this book are used when one grappler is standing and the other is on his knees. These "transition" moves from groundfighting to standing situations are seen in every style of sport combat grappling and in self-defense situations as well.

There hasn't been much published on this phase of groundfighting and I hope this book fills that void. Also, I use the term "guard" when describing fighting from the back or buttocks. This is a fairly new term, made popular in the 1990s and is very much part the common terminology used in groundfighting today. If you're a history buff (as I am), the Japanese judo exponents who developed the concepts and core skills of fighting on the mat originally (and still do) called groundfighting "newaza." I've mentioned this word before, but a close examination of it shows the unique approach the early judo men took to grappling. The word "ne" means to recline or lay down. "Waza" means technique. This distinctive word illustrates the importance the Japanese gave for fighting off the buttocks/back in judo. Additionally, any method of breaking down or turning over an opponent, or getting past his legs (passing the guard) or rolling him over (sweeping from the guard) was called "newaza no semekata" (forms of attacking in groundfighting). While this may seem trivial, it really hits home how the Japanese viewed grappling on the mat or ground and gives us a clear idea of why and how groundfighting as we do it today was conceptualized and developed.

As with all of my books, the skills presented have been tested on mats all over the world. Show-off moves may work on somebody who doesn't have a clue how to grapple, but my intention is to teach skills that have stood the test of both time and competition. I've often told my athletes; "If you only prepare to catch only the fish, the sharks will eat you." Also, this isn't the complete or final word on this subject. An author can't possibly present everything he knows in a book or series of books, and no author knows everything there is about any given subject. I've tried to show skills that have a high ratio of success in real situations and how and why they work. The skills shown in this book are my particular approach to groundfighting and based on real-world experience. What may appear to be the same technique to an untrained observer often has many levels of application and purpose. A truly skilled exponent of sport combat and grappling values the fundamentals and how to personalize them so they work against serious, skilled and fit opponents.

Fundamental concepts of movement and position are featured in all of my books and this book is no different. This is done so that anyone who studies this book will know not only how to make a move work, but why it works. When you understand why something works, then you can make it work in a variety of situations with a higher ratio of success. Not only that, when you understand why a technique works (and the underlying, fundamental principles of the technique), you will be better able to take that technique to a higher level of skill and application against a skilled, serious, physically fit and resisting opponent. Skill is the practical application of technique. The skills shown in this book range from the basic to the complex, and the common thread among them all is that they are practical and can be adapted to make them fit your style. Don't hesitate to change anything you see in this book to make it work for you.

I will use the word "pin" throughout this book. When a pin is discussed, it's in the context of a hold-down or immobilization as we use in judo, jujitsu, submission grappling, sambo and mixed martial arts rather than in the western sense of pinning an opponent's shoulders to the mat. I will also use the word "groundfighting" in this book. Groundfighting is a generic word that can simply mean grappling or actually mean using strikes and punches. In almost every situation shown in this book, you can easily follow up with striking techniques or use these skills in the sport grappling sense.

Winning At Groundfighting

The point of this book is that grappling on the mat takes place in many positions and from many situations. To be a champion in any grappling sport, you have to master the core, fundamental skills and master how to control the position. After doing that, you must have an arsenal of skills and moves from a variety of positions where you can put your opponent into a position of vulnerability. The key positions from which I will use to break an opponent down are:

• When you are on your knees with your opponent on his hands and knees and you are at his side.

• When you are on your knees with your opponent on his hands and knees and you are at his head.

• When your opponent is on all fours and you are in the rodeo ride position where you control him with your legs.

• When your opponent is flat on his front in what I call the "chicken" position.

• When you are on all fours and your opponent is on his knees to your side in the wrestler's ride position.

• When you are on all fours and your opponent is on his knees at your head.

• When both you and your opponent are on your knees.

• When you are standing and your opponent is on both or one of his knees.

• When you are on your knees and your opponent is standing.

• When you are fighting off your buttocks, hips or backside with your opponent between your legs in the guard position or when you are on your back and your opponent is on top of you in the mount position.

• When you are on your knees between your opponent's legs in his guard position.

In much the same way it was when I started judo in the 1960s, fighting from the buttocks in what has become known as the guard is used extensively in many forms of jujitsu and submission grappling. There are many good books on the market that deal exclusively with this phase of groundfighting. The guard is a viable, technically sound position to fight from and is an integral part of grappling, but this book's emphasis is to present a broad view of successful groundfighting and grappling. I've included in this book skills from the guard position that are effective and can be used by a variety of grapplers, no matter the strength level or weight class. However, the breakdowns in this book represent grappling and groundfighting from a variety of positions and situations and from a variety of grappling sports. A breakdown is very much like a throw. One instant your opponent is stable and secure, and then he's on his back. You put him there. Good breakdowns require plyometric power and explosiveness. Sure, there are times when you roll your opponent onto his back in an almost gradual or incremental way, but usually you break him down or roll him onto his back with sudden and controlled force, much like you do when you throw him from a standing position onto his back.

With this analogy to throws, I believe you have to perform a breakdown using the same principles you would when you throw an opponent. You actually break an opponent's balance when you break him down for a pin in much the same way you would if you throw him. There are several phases to a breakdown, regardless of your starting position or your opponent's starting position. He can be on his knees, in your guard, or any groundfighting position, and these principles of making a breakdown work come into play.

1. **Grip:** Control your opponent by how you grab him and how you use the handles on his (and your) body or grappling uniform.

2. **Control your opponent's Position/Balance:** By controlling how he moves, you dictate the terms of the fight. You break your opponent's balance by taking his supporting arm, leg, knee (or any body part), from him. Breaking down a human body is like breaking down a table. If you pull in one of the supporting legs of a table, it will collapse. So will a human body. You have to fit your body into a position so you are better able to

control your opponent and break him down.

3. **Execute your specific breakdown:** This is when you manipulate and use your arms, hands, legs and feet as well as body position to perform the actual breakdown. At this point, you are breaking your opponent down and getting him to the position you want him to be in.

4. **Finish:** You've followed through from the breakdown and have him in the pin. At this point, you tighten the control of the pin and immobilize him. From here, you can decide what you want to do if you choose to go for a submission technique or (in MMA or a real fight) possibly even punch or kick him.

If you want to be a complete grappler or fighter, I recommend the Shingitai approach as your basis of training. The name "Shingitai" is comprised of three separate words (and concepts) and when done together, form a great philosophy of training.

1. **Shin:** This Japanese word translates to mean, "fighting heart." To be successful in a fighting sport or martial discipline, you must have the will to not only win, but also enjoy the rough and tumble activity you are engaged in. This doesn't mean you need to be the toughest guy in the world, but it does mean you should be tough enough to get the job done. The words of the famous lawman of the old west Bat Masterson are true; "It's not always the fastest or most accurate, it's the most willing."

2. **Gi:** This Japanese word translates to mean "applied technical ability." This is what skill is. You have to be skillful and know how and why your skills work best for you. You can win by brute force, luck or other factors for only so long and against only a limited level of competition. My first sambo coach, Maurice Allen, told me; "Make the technique work for you." If you want to be a champion, you have to be able to apply the techniques and make them work for you.

3. **Tai:** This actually means "body" and anything relating to the body. For our purposes, it means physical fitness. "Show up in shape" is a phrase you should live by as a grappler. The great football coach Vince Lombardi said; "Physical weakness makes cowards of us all." If you want to perform any skill against a resisting, serious, physically fit and skilled opponent, you must be physically capable of doing it.

As I've said before, the skills and ideas presented in this book have withstood both the tests of time and competition. Techniques, like music and fashion, come in and out of style. However, the desire to win never seems to go out of style and the skills in this book can definitely be part of your overall approach to winning.

Making Pins And Breakdowns Intinctive

The best way to be able to break an opponent down and pin him when you need to in a real situation is to drill on it so much that it becomes instinctive behavior. You shouldn't have to "think through" what you're doing. By the time you've thought it through, your opponent has escaped or reversed the situation, and your opportunity to pin him has been lost.

Before you can drill on moves, every athlete needs good coaching. There are a lot of good coaches teaching good skills, so make it a point to seek one out and learn from him. A vital key to your development as an athlete is a good coach. Your grit and determination will take you a long way, but a good

coach will make that journey a lot easier. While you most likely will have one person who you will recognize as your main coach, there will be a lot of people along the way that you can, and will, learn from. This photo shows the author, Steve Scott, coaching his athletes at a typical workout.

Mat Uchikomi (Fitting Practice or Repetition Practice)

Training on a consistent basis with discipline and forethought is what separates a champion from a tough guy who likes to roll around with his buddies. Drill training is essential for learning skills and making them work for you. Spend a large amount of time every practice in drilling on your moves in addition to going live or randori.

A great way to practice breakdowns and pins is to do what are called "uchikomi." Uchikomi is repetition training. Doing the move over and over again with different levels of resistance until you can do it in your sleep.

When drill-training on breakdowns and pins (or any skill for that matter), the primary rule is: "Correct practice develops a correct skill." If you don't practice the moves correctly, then you won't be able to actually perform the move when you need to. You can work really hard and do hundreds of repetitions of any technique, but if you don't practice the mechanically correct form of that technique, it will simply reinforce a bad technique. Also, don't simply go through the motions or do the drills to get it over with. Train with a purpose, even if it's simply for the joy of learning (and doing) a move with extreme skill.

Remember, when you practice, it's practice. That may seem like a dumb thing to say, but working out on the mat isn't a match. There is plenty of time for randori or free grappling later in the workout, but make sure you spend a good amount of time working on your skills and drill training. People who don't understand how to train efficiently often think the only way to work out is to go full-blast in free grappling during every practice. Doing this type of training leads to a quick burnout, injuries and getting (and staying) stuck in a rut from a technical perspective. If you want to improve your skill, fitness level and fighting spirit, follow a disciplined regimen of training that includes drill training. I've followed a simple formula for workouts for many years with great success. A typical training session is divided into three main parts. They are:

1. **Warm-ups and drill training:** This is the time whey the group does various exercises, games and calisthenics to warm the body up, then some functional stretching. This is followed by the coach running the group through specific drills to reinforce skills, fitness and tactics as well as develop moves instinctively.

2. **Skill training:** This is the part of the workout when the coach teaches new skills or works on previously learned moves. The group practices the skills the coach wants them to and may even do some drills to reinforce the move just learned.

3. **Randori (Free Grappling):** The group now has time to "go live" and work out in practice grappling. This is practice time, not a tournament.

In training, you will take falls, get tapped out or pinned and you will do the same to your partners. They're partners, not opponents.

If you can work out on a consistent basis with good training partners and with a coach that not only encourages you, but also can teach you, then you're in a good place. Appreciate what you have and make the most of it. If you're missing any part of the above, try to make improvements in your training situation. The bottom line is that if you want to perform to the best of your ability, you not only have to train hard, but you also have to train smart.

SECTION ONE:
Position, Then Pin

"Impose your will on your opponent. Make him fight your kind of fight."

Steve Scott

Before you can pin your opponent, you have to control his body. The better you limit his movement by controlling his legs, hips, arms and pretty much everything about your opponent, the better you will be able to pin him.

If you've read my other books, you know that I am a firm believer in controlling the position. Position is being in the right place at the right time and putting your opponent in the wrong place (for him) every time. You want to limit his movement, limit his options and nullify what he can do. Not only do you want to limit his movement, you should try to "shut him down" so that he can't put you in a bad position.

I've tried to show a number of positions common to every form of submission grappling and wrestling practiced in this section. Good grappling is moving from one position to another position to even another position and trying to control your opponent and ultimately make him give up to you.

Also shown are some common sense tips that are necessary for effective and reliable pins and breakdowns. This is the kind of information that separates an athlete who knows what he wants and how to get it from the athlete who wishes he had trained harder and smarter in the gym. Some of these tips may seem pretty obvious, but don't neglect them or take them for granted. They can be good friends to you when you need them!

A Good Base

In the same way a solid house is built, a solid pin needs a good foundation. Your lower body often supplies that foundation, so it's important to keep your hips low, knees wide and feet dug into the mat when pinning your opponent. This photo shows Steve holding Greg and relying on a solid base to make it work.

Post a Leg, Arm or your Head for Balance

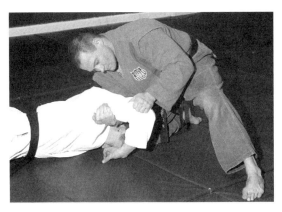

Bryan is posting his leg wide to maintain balance and a good base. Sometimes, you may have to place your head on the mat or support your weight with your arm for better balance and control. Posting is another part of providing yourself with a good, solid, base.

Wrestler's Ride (Get His Back)

A good rule of thumb is to always try to get behind your opponent and don't allow him to get behind you. If he can't see you, you have a better chance of setting him up for a breakdown. Notice how Bill "has his opponent's back" and is gripping Steve's lapel for better control of his upper body. Bill is controlling Steve by staying slightly behind Steve's right hip and controlling Steve's hips and lower body. Bill stays on his toes as shown and constantly keeps close contact with his opponent's back and hip with his own chest. By staying on his toes, Bill is mobile and can move freely. He also makes sure to use his weight and body movement to limit Steve's movement. Whenever Steve moves, Bill exerts pressure to control where Steve goes. Bill can use this position as a good start to further work another position and gain more control over Steve's body. If you're the grappler riding your opponent, you have a distinct and decided advantage and can work a lot of set-ups from this position.

Don't Let Your Opponent Shrimp into You

The best time to escape from a hold is the second you know you've been had and the best way to escape is to quickly shrimp into your opponent. John is preventing Eric from shrimping into him and starting his escape. John has posted his right hand on the mat under Eric's right hip and upper leg. This keeps Eric from curling his right leg and turning onto his right hip to start his escape.

Nick, on top, is keeping Kirt from shrimping in to start his escape by jamming his right knee in and under Kirt's near (in this case, right) hip. Nick is using his right knee in the same way John used his right arm to block the bottom grappler from turning in and starting his escape.

27

Chicken Position

When your opponent is laying flat on his front with his arms tucked in or up around his neck, he's telling you a lot about his lack of ability in groundfighting! This is what I call the "chicken position." It's a weak position on the mat and not one I recommend! As you can see in this photo, the bottom man, Eric, is laying flat on his face and pretty much at the mercy of Steve, who is about to yank up on his belt and dig in for a choke. This position is taken by an opponent who is very defensive, is usually not skilled in groundfighting or may be tired and trying to take a rest. No matter why he gets in this position, it's a bad thing for him if the top grappler knows what to do! The bottom man in the chicken position lays flat on his face much like an ostrich who sticks his head in the sand and hopes a threat will go away. The threat doesn't go away, he simply takes advantage of the grappler who hides like this and sets him up for a submission hold! If you're the top grappler, you might want to say a silent thank you when your opponent lays flat in the chicken position. Sometimes, an opponent may roll over onto his front after you have thrown him trying to lessen the score of the throw. This is also a good time to take advantage of this chicken position. There is usually no real good reason to end up in the chicken position other than temporarily being there to see what your opponent might do.

Top (Standing) Ride

This is a ride position that is similar to the wrestler's ride, but the attacker is more upright with his knees off the mat. The idea in this position is to get behind your opponent and quickly dig your feet in. As soon as you get behind your opponent, immediately dig your leg (or legs) in and control his hips. There are many options the top grappler can do from this position. He can work his legs in and secure a rodeo ride, work immediately into a rolling strangle or flatten the bottom man out onto his face and stomach into the chicken position. The important thing is that the top grappler, Steve, should immediately work behind his opponent as shown so that he can control the position better.

Bottom Position on Elbows and Knees

Notice in this photo that the bottom man, Bill, is on his elbows and knees and not on his hands and knees. It's wise for the bottom grappler to be in this position and not straighten his arms. Bill is in a bad position and knows it, so to increase his chances of getting out of this position and out of trouble, he keeps his arms bent, close to his body, hips as low as possible and stays on his toes so he can move quickly to initiate a way to get from the bottom.

Rodeo Ride (Get Your Hooks In)

The rodeo ride is one of the best positions possible to set an opponent up for a pin. This is a position you should work on and work on a lot! You have almost total control of your opponent's body and something as equally important…you have his back! The rodeo ride (shown in this photo) is achieved when the top wrestler has successfully gone behind his opponent, dug his feet in his opponent's crotch and "got his back." Bill, on top, has his hooks in and dug his feet into Steve's hips and crotch. Bill is controlling Steve's lower body well and is careful to not hook his feet together at the ankles, as this doesn't give as much control of his opponent's body. Bill has hooked under Steve's arms for upper body control as well. The rodeo ride is a good example of "leg wrestling."

As I've mentioned before, you have to control your opponent's body before you work your pin in on him. Usually, if you control your opponent's lower extremities (his hips and legs) to set him up and control him. Notice that Bill, the top grappler, has Steve firmly in control. Bill has excellent leg control with "his hooks in," meaning he has his legs in Steve's crotch area and controlling his entire lower body. As said earlier, it's important not to hook your ankles as this limits your ability to manipulate and control your opponent with your feet. The rodeo ride is a strong position no matter what style of grappling you use it in.

Seated Rodeo Ride

Here's a rodeo ride where both grapplers are seated on the mat. The grappler in back, Steve, may want to roll Bret onto his buttocks as shown here. Steve can control Bret from this position for a while and start working for a breakdown from this position. We have several moves later in the book using this position.

Rodeo Ride Using the Triangle

A powerful way to control your opponent when you are in the rodeo ride is to wrap your legs around his waist and get him in a triangle. You can dominate the position for a long time and set the bottom grappler up for a submission technique or work him into a pin.

Rodeo Ride and Flatten Opponent:
Control Your Opponent's Lower Body

Steve has flattened Bill out and broken him down from Bill's initial position on his elbows and knees. Notice how Steve has dug his legs in deep and is controlling Bill's lower body. Steve is rocking Bill forward to prevent Bill from getting his knees and feet down to try to escape. This is a strong position for the top grappler! As a continuation of the rodeo ride, in almost every aspect of groundfighting, you need to control your opponent's lower body (his hips and legs) before you can break him down further and get him on his back. If you don't, he can shuck you off or escape easily. By controlling your opponent's lower body, you have good control of his entire body.

Stay Round

Quite often, you will have to roll your opponent into position to pin him. For this reason, make it a habit to "stay round." Work on your flexibility so that you can roll in most any direction with ease to control your opponent.

Fighting From the Bottom (Guard)

Many grapplers may prefer to fight from this position, and if you do, make sure that you are active and aggressive. This is an old position from the early days of judo and it has stood the test of time. Notice that the grappler on the right in the photo, Bill, is on his buttocks and using his feet and legs as if they were his arms. He is controlling Steve with his left foot in Steve's hip and his right foot on Steve's thigh. The rule of thumb is that if the grappler who is in the guard wants to be aggressive, he should close the space between the two bodies and if he wants to be defensive, he should open the space and attempt to escape or get to his feet. While this is often true, sometimes the bottom grappler may close the space to keep his opponent from doing too much.

Protect Your Middle Area

When fighting off of your buttocks, back and hips in the guard position make sure you protect the middle part of your body. Keep your opponent from getting past your hips. Use your feet, legs, knees, hands, arms and elbows to manipulate your opponent and control the space. If your opponent gets past your knees, he can pass your guard and start to control you.

Follow Through from a Throw or Takedown

Following through to a pin after throwing or taking down your opponent can be your "insurance" to make sure your opponent is beaten. Always follow through to the ground after you throw an opponent!

Leg Press Position

This is a stabilizing position that the top grappler takes when he rolls his opponent over onto his back. While this position is used mostly for the cross-body armlock, it's still a good one to set up some pins (such as the straddle pin) with as well. Notice how Bill, on top, is sitting on his buttocks right by Josh's shoulder and pressing with his legs. The bottom grappler's shoulder and upper arm are planted in the top wrestler's crotch. Bill controls Josh by squeezing his knees together and hooking his ankles (not always needed). Bill is pulling in with his feet on Josh's far shoulder, causing it to "accordion." This keeps the bottom wrestler from getting his shoulders square or stable. Bill got to this position by rolling Josh onto his back and will attempt to lever or pry his opponent's arm loose to secure the submission. The top grappler may not stay in this position very long, or he may keep the bottom man there for some time. This is a common, and useful, position and almost always gives the top grappler a stable position to secure a submission or continue on to a hold-down.

Control Your Opponent's Head

Most pins have one major thing in common: you have to control your opponent's head to secure the hold tightly. Whether you are hooking an arm under your opponent's head to create more control or trapping it in some other way to keep your opponent from using his head to bridge and escape, by limiting the movement of your opponent's head, you will control the rest of his body with greater effectiveness. Nick is hooking his right arm under Kirt's head to keep Kirt from bridging to start an escape and to trap Kirt's head to insure greater control of the rest of Kirt's body.

John is controlling Chance's head by using his right hand to grab Chance's collar and pulling it in tight to him. As John does this, he drives his right upper arm into Chance's head and uses his right arm like a nutcracker squeezing a nut. This can sometimes cause an opponent to tap out from the pressure on his head and neck.

Here's another way of trapping your opponent's head. If your opponent has shot in for a takedown or you end up at his head as shown here, keep his head down and pinched between your legs. Don't let him pop his head out to one side or another because he can start working a breakdown on you from the bottom. Steve, on top, can start working a breakdown on Nick from this position.

Control the Space

It's important to be aware of how close or how far you are from your opponent. You need "working room" to maneuver into a set-up or defensive action against your opponent. Usually, if you are the aggressor, you will want to close the distance between you and your opponent and if you are the defender, you will want to increase the space between your two bodies. While this is generally true, it's not always the case and in some instances you may have to close into your opponent tightly to keep him from applying a move on you.

Close the Guard

Here's an example of the "closed guard" position that is often used to control the top grappler when fighting off the back or guard position. In this case, Bill, the bottom man, is trapping Ben to his body with his legs preventing him from attacking and giving Bill a chance to asses the situation and work a move from the bottom. Bill's keeping Ben in close and tight, which gives Bill some time and opportunity to either catch a breath or methodically work for a scoring move. This position is a good example of controlling the space, which in turn, controls your opponent.

Here is another example of a closed guard position. Steve has Kelly in his closed guard and is using a body triangle to control Kelly's body. Steve, on the bottom, is applying some serious pressure on Kelly's ribs and torso, all the while controlling the position with both his legs and using his hands to keep Kelly's upper body controlled.

Use Your Feet and Legs Like Your Hands and Arms

Josh is using his feet and legs to control and manipulate Travis's hips and is using his feet as if they were his hands to manipulate and move his opponent. If you think of your feet and legs as you do your hands and arms when grappling, you will use them more effectively.

Leg Wrestling

Here's an example of leg wrestling. Bret is manipulating and controlling Eric's body with his leg and sinking in a near leg ride. By good use of leg wrestling, Bret has controlled Eric's body and position so that he can break Eric down further or roll him into a pinning situation more effectively. Using your legs to control and manipulate your opponent is an important skill. Such positions as the rodeo ride and the guard emphasize the use of leg wrestling. Leg wrestling is basically using your legs and feet as if they were your arms and hands. Use your feet and legs as you would your hands and arms to manipulate your opponent's body.

Hand and Arm Wrestling

Controlling your opponent's hands and arms is crucial in setting him up and making him tap out. As with leg wrestling, you have to use your limbs (in this case your upper extremities) to control and manipulate your opponent. This photo shows John using one hand to control Chance's arm and the other hand to control chance at the belt.

Use Your Hands Independently

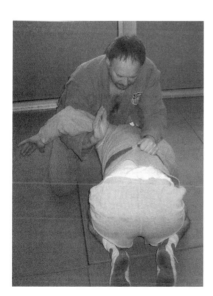

Each of your hands has a specific job in breaking down your opponent. Be aware of how to use your hands to control and manipulate your opponent's jacket, arms, legs or any part of him (or you) that will control him. This is all part of the "hand wrestling" I described. Here, Steve is using his right arm to hook under Shawn's left shoulder as Steve controls Shawn's body by grabbing his belt with his left hand.

Patience is a Virtue

Work methodically and don't rush things. Go logically and methodically from step A to step B to step C and don't skip any steps. I always like to tell my athletes; "Take your time, but do it in hurry!" What I mean is to work methodically, but don't dawdle. Be as efficient as possible in your body movement and get the job done. Good groundfighting isn't flashy or fancy. It's "blue collar" grappling in the truest sense!

One Thing Leads to Another

What my good friend, Jim Schneweis, calls "action-reaction-action." It's also called "chain wrestling." Jake is moving from a straddle pin to a vertical pin, all the while keeping good control over Josh. Jake reacted to Josh's escape and is linking moves together in some good chain wrestling.

Never Reach too Far (Don't Extend Yourself too Far)

Don't be so concerned about getting your hands on your opponent's upper body that you reach too far. Don't rush in without measuring the situation. If you extend your arms too far, your opponent could take your extended arm and work in an armlock. As often as not, groundfighting is a waiting game and your opponent may wait for you to do something foolish by trying to force the action before thinking! Control his lower body, including both his legs and hips. If you're in the top position and your opponent is in the guard, don't let him suck you into a tight clinch or closed guard situation. Give yourself both time and room to work. However, sometimes you will have to extend your arm or arms to grip your opponent or secure a better position or get a better hold of your opponent. But when you do, make sure you are in a good position and don't rush in without a plan.

Make it Uncomfortable

Sometimes, you have to distract your opponent by causing some physical discomfort to make a move work. It's not always the case, but there are some definite situations where you have to distract your opponent so that you can break him down or make the pin so uncomfortable when you apply it, all he can think about is how much it hurts. In this photo, Steve has his right shoulder jammed under Eric's neck and has his chin driving hard into Eric's collarbone to better control Eric. Submission grappling, judo, jujitsu, sambo, mixed martial arts and other forms of personal combat are physically hard. You have to do what is necessary to get the job done. Like they say, it's the price of doing business!

Everything is a Handle

Consider every part of your opponent's body and workout uniform as if it is a handle. In fact, use any and every part of your own body and attire as you would a handle! In this photo, Bret has grabbed Eric's upper leg and is using it to turn him onto his back for a banana split.

Apply Constant Pressure

Groundfighting is the epitome of putting pressure on your opponent! Work for your best position, then work for the best set up or breakdown and keep creating opportunities to choke him out. Don't let up on him; grind him and make him dislike every second he's on the mat with you. Even if he manages to get away, make him wish he had never seen you. Some call it "ground and pound" but I like to call it "blue collar groundfighting." There's nothing fancy or pretty about it, but it gets the job done. In this photo, Jake has rolled Josh over onto his back and is using his right knee to apply pressure and control on Josh's torso. Jake can hold Josh with the straddle pin or use this position temporarily for control and work to another hold.

SECTION TWO:
The Core Pins

"Plant him there until he quits."
Shawn Watson, U.S. National Champion in Judo, Sambo and Sport Jujitsu

There are specific core, primary pins and holds that are used in almost every style of grappling and wrestling. Each of these core pinning techniques has a variety of modifications and variations that is limited only by our imagination. This section presents these core skills of pinning and these are the pins that will be featured throughout this book. These core pins are the ones I teach my athletes who train in Shingitai Jujitsu, judo and sambo with me. In later sections, I will discuss various breakdowns, set-ups and escapes that have proven effective in competitive situations. Depending on the rules of your combat sport, some may be more useful than others, but each of these core pinning techniques do the job for which they are intended; they will hold your opponent to the mat or ground, and if done well, hold him for as long as you want him there. As Shawn Watson so aptly said, "Plant him there until he quits."

The Essentials of Every Good Pin

Every good pin has qualities that make it work. As I point out in the following checklist, a pin is simply a strong, dominant position you have over your opponent while you are restraining him and immobilizing the movement of his body. There are essential areas of control and movement that you must exert over your opponent to keep him restrained on the mat. All of these essentials are illustrated in the first section of this book, but this quick checklist might be helpful.

1. **Head control.** Control your opponent's head so he can't bridge out of your pin. In most cases, the body follows where the head goes. If the head is stuck, the body is usually stuck too.

2. **Have a good base with your legs and hips.** Keep your knees wide and use the weight of your legs and lower body to counter-balance the pressure you're putting on him with your upper body.

3. **Keep your hips low to the mat usually.** If you keep your hips low to the mat, this inhibits your opponent's movement.

4. **Have good torso contact.** Whether it's chest-to-chest, chest to upper body, the side of your body to his body, or any torso contact, make sure it's secure and tight. Try to make your body and your opponent's body

as tightly connected together as possible.

5. **Mobility is important.** Be ready to shift your body weight, switch leg or hip position or even switch to another pin or submission technique. A good pin is simply a strong, dominant position that restrains and immobilizes your opponent's movement. If you understand this, you will have good success in pinning.

6. **Keep your body weight centered and balanced.** Remember, you have to hold this guy down to the mat for a while. This point flows naturally from #5.

7. **Use your hands effectively.** This ties in with #8, but make sure to grab anything you can (that's allowed in the rules of your grappling sport) to control him.

8. **Everything is a handle.** Use any part of your opponent's body or clothing, as well as your own, to control him.

9. **Make the pin uncomfortable for your opponent.** Apply constant pressure on your opponent. You want pain, or even the act of being uncomfortable, to be foremost in his thoughts. If he's tied up in a knot, a quick escape isn't usually the first thing he thinks of.

10. **You're the guy winning.** You're pinning him. Remember that and keep him there. Don't do anything unnecessary that might give him a chance to escape. You may not be beating him with a cool submission technique or earth-shattering throw, but you're beating him all the same. Years ago, when I was a young man and fighting in a regional judo tournament, I pinned a guy and what he said after the match stuck in my mind. He told me; "You only pinned me. You couldn't throw me." My reply wasn't intended to be a clever or smart comeback. I simply reacted honestly. I told him; "But I still won." Enough said.

The Chest Hold

The primary pin I teach to athletes is the chest hold, called "mune gatame" in Japanese. I consider it to be the most fundamental of all pins for the simple fact that it is very effective and demonstrates just about every good thing there is to know about holding an opponent on the mat and not letting him up. This is also a fairly easy pin to teach beginners, but (like so many skills) it's such an effective pin that it's used in world-class judo, sambo and submission grappling events as well. The chest hold is a strong, stable pin that is hard to escape from and allows the athlete applying the pin excellent mobility so he can switch to another pin or make adjustments to retain control when needed. Other pins are shown as well, and all are useful and effective. This section shows a fundamental application of each pin, and later in the book, you will see a number of variations and different applications of the core pins presented as a follow-up from a breakdown. However, many breakdowns and rollovers in this book will end in a chest hold. It's a personal preference of mine based on winning results over the years. I encourage and highly recommend that you to develop a strong chest hold, and then branch out from there depending on your grappling sport or personal preference.

Chest Hold (Basic Position)

Chris has his hips low and knees wide and makes sure to keep his buttocks as low to the mat as possible. His feet are dug into the mat for mobility. Chris has his left knee jammed under Bob's right shoulder and has his left arm hooked under Bob's head to prevent him from bridging. Chris has hugged Bob and is squeezing hard with both of his arms with solid chest-to-chest contact. Chris may have to change his leg, hip or torso position, and his goal is to keep Bob as flat on his back as possible with that strong chest-to-chest contact.

Chest Hold (Legs Extended)

This shows how Chris can extend his legs, lengthening his base. Chris makes it a point to keep his hips low to the mat for better balance.

Chest Hold (Sit-through)

This is still the chest hold, but Chris has done a sit-through, with his right leg forward.

Chest Hold (Riding High)

This chest hold shows Steve with a strong chest-to-chest position, but with his legs extended wide and his hips high. This form of the chest hold relies on strong arm control over your opponent to ride him and restrain him.

Sambo Chest Hold

This is a common hold in sambo and shows Ben holding Bill. Ben is basically in Bill's guard, but has made strong torso-to-torso contact and Ben is holding Bill to the mat, waiting for a chance to work a submission technique.

Chest Hold (also called the Hip Hold)

This is a variation of the chest hold called the hip hold or "koshi gatame" in Japanese. Steve is holding John in the same way he would in a standard chest hold except that he is holding lower on John's body at the hips. Steve has hugged John's body at the hips and has jammed his left knee under John's left buttocks. Not a common pin, but it works!

The Side Hold

One of the standard pins in all forms of grappling. Steve is holding Eric from the side and has used his left hand to hook under Eric's neck, keeping it from touching the mat and preventing Eric from bridging. Steve has strong torso-to-torso contact and has reached his right arm through Eric's legs to control his hips and lower body. There are many variations of this pin.

The Upper Body (or Upper Chest) Hold

Also called the "north south" position, this is an extremely effective pin and one that has many variations. I recommend that everyone learn and master this pin, then explore the almost countless variations of it from a variety of breakdowns and situations.

The Upper Body Hold (Legs Extended)

John has extended his legs to widen his lower body support while holding Eric.

The Vertical Hold (Pin)

Mike is holding Steve by controlling Steve's upper body at the head and shoulders with his arms and laying length-wise on him. Mike's knees are wide for balance and support and his feet are tucked under Steve's buttocks.

The Mount

This is an adaptation of the vertical hold and is useful in mixed martial arts and self-defense. Bryan, on top, can hold Jarrod down for a long time by shifting his body weight and riding him. This position is extremely useful and a variety of submission techniques can be used from this pin.

This is a strong hold. Bryan can easily start striking Jarrod, and as any fan of mixed martial arts knows, the bottom guy is in serious trouble!

The Scarf Hold (Head and Arm Pin)

Steve is holding Bill from the side using his right arm looped around Bill's neck and head. (This is why the Japanese named this hold the "scarf" hold.) Steve is using his left hand and arm to control Bill's right arm. Steve has a strong base with his hips and legs and he keeps his center of gravity low so he can hold Bill to the mat.

The Straddle Pin

Steve is holding Greg from the side by jamming his right knee in Greg's torso at the stomach, ribs or chest. Steve is using his left hand to control Greg's neck and using his right arm to control Greg's legs and hips. Notice that Steve has posted his left foot out far for balance. This is a painful hold for the bottom grappler and allows Steve a lot of mobility, making a follow-up with a submission technique a real possibility.

The Shoulder Lock Pin

This is a strong pin, but is also a great double trouble move in that Bill, on top, can apply a strong choke on Steve as well. Bill makes sure to jam his head into Steve's upper arm and shoulder as he squeezes tight with his arms. Bill has locked his hands together tightly and has his right knee jammed in Steve's backside right under Steve's right shoulder. Bill's left leg is posted out straight and is used as a counter balance to maintain a strong base. A variation of this pin, called the body scissors shoulder lock is shown later in this book.

The Upper Back Pin

This is a variation of the old judo pin called "ura gatame" which means rear or backside hold. This hold usually comes out of the banana split breakdown and is used in freestyle and collegiate wrestling, but certainly is useful in any style of grappling.

The Triangle Pin

Using your legs to form a triangle on your opponent's shoulders and upper body is a strong way to pin him. Kirk is using a standard from of the triangle pin on Travis. Basically, Kirk has formed a triangle with his legs on Travis's left shoulder and head and has used his left arm to hook around Travis's upper left leg.

Rear Scarf Hold

This is a useful and strong pin. John has used his left arm to hook under Eric's head and is using his right arm to hold Eric's right arm (at the elbow) tightly to his body. John's left hip is wedged under Eric's right shoulder and John is using his left leg as a rudder or steering leg while his right leg is the power leg as he pushes off the mat with his right foot. John's wide base with his legs gives him excellent balance. This is a great pin.

SECTION THREE:
Breakdowns

"Hence the skillful fighter puts himself into a position that makes defeat impossible and does not miss the moment for defeating the enemy."
Sun Tzu

Breakdowns and Their Importance In Grappling

Breaking your opponent down from a stable to an unstable position, then applying a pin or finishing hold is what grappling is all about. I believe the value of breakdowns in winning on the mat is so important; these moves take up a majority of pages in this book. A breakdown is any move that puts you in a superior position to your opponent and sets him up for a finishing hold. I often compare breakdowns to throws. Another way of saying it is that breakdowns are throws done from a groundfighting perspective. As explained in the introduction to this book, no opponent is going to lie down and let you pin him. You have to put him on his back first, and the better you are at doing it, the better chance you have of pinning him.

Some people call these moves "turnovers" but I prefer to call these techniques breakdowns because that's exactly what you are doing. You don't always turn an opponent over, but you always break him down. The name breakdown implies an aggressive and dominant act and in any sport or activity associated with grappling, being aggressive is often a good thing. Breakdowns are done from any position, no matter what position you are in or what position your opponent is in. Any move that takes your opponent from a stable position to an unstable position is a breakdown, no matter if he is kneeling, flat on his face, sitting on his buttocks, sitting between your legs or any of the many positions we find ourselves in when we engage in sport combat on the mat. Groundfighting and grappling puts you in many positions and situations. The better you know how to fight from these situations, the better chance you have of winning.

In this book's introduction, I discussed the various positions where breakdowns will be used in this book. For easy reference, they are listed here as well. The key positions from which I will use to break an opponent down are:

• When you are on your knees with your opponent on his hands and knees and you are at his side.

• When you are on your knees with your opponent on his hands and knees and you are at his head.

• When your opponent is on all fours and you are in the rodeo ride position where you control him with your legs.

- When your opponent is flat on his front in what I call the "chicken" position.

- When you are on all fours and your opponent is on his knees to your side in the wrestler's ride position.

- When you are on all fours and your opponent is on his knees at your head.

- When both you and your opponent are on your knees.

- When you are standing and your opponent is on both or one of his knees.

- When you are on your knees and your opponent is standing.

- When you are fighting off your buttocks, hips or backside with your opponent between your legs in the guard position or when you are on your back and your opponent is on top of you in the mount position.

- When you are on your knees between your opponent's legs in his guard position.

Far Arm-Near Leg Breakdown to Chest Hold

This is a fundamental skill and works at all levels of competition. Steve is at the side of Greg and on his knees. Greg is on all fours.

Steve uses the arm closest to Greg's head (the left arm in this photo) and grabs Greg's far (in this case, right) elbow. Steve makes sure to use his hand like a hook for better control. Steve's upper chest is pushing against the left side of Greg's body.

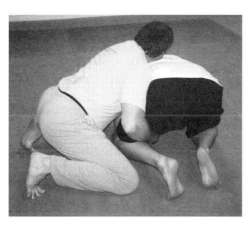

Here is a rear view of the move. Steve is using his right arm to grab around Greg's left upper leg. Steve's right shoulder is firmly pressed against Greg's left hip and Steve's head is on Greg's back as shown.

Steve uses his left hand to pull in on Greg's far (right) elbow as Steve uses his right arm to lift Greg's near (left) leg. Steve rolls Greg over his shoulder as shown. Notice that Steve's upper chest is firmly pushing against Greg's body.

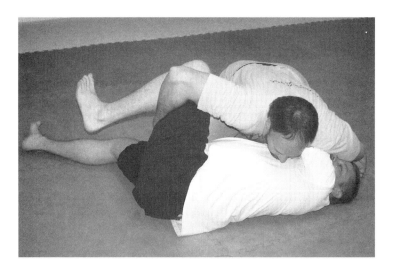

Steve has rolled Greg over onto his back and is over on top of him. Steve keeps control with his hands and arms until Greg is completely on his back.

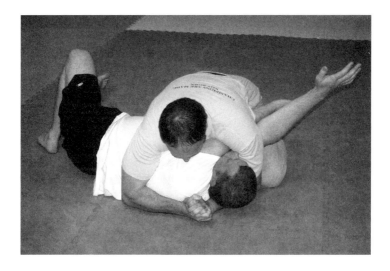

Steve immediately goes into a chest hold. In this case, Steve has trapped both of Greg's arms.

Steve may end up in a chest hold with his arm under Greg's neck and not trap his arms. Either way, Greg is on his back with Steve pinning him.

Both Elbows Breakdown to Chest Hold

This is a variation of the far arm near leg breakdown.

Steve uses both hands to scoop Greg's far (in this case right) arm and pull it into Steve. Notice that Steve has one hand over the other and hasn't laced his fingers. Steve's upper chest is driving into Greg's side.

Steve drives hard and scoops both of Greg's arms as he does, forcing Greg to roll to his back.

Steve finishes with a chest hold.

Double Leg Breakdown to Chest Hold

Here's another variation of the far arm near leg breakdown. Steve is using both of his hands and arms to scoop Greg's far knee and leg as shown. Steve's upper chest is driving hard into Greg's hip.

Steve drives hard and uses both hands to scoop Greg's legs together and collapse him onto his side. Steve makes sure to not let go of Greg's legs or he might lose control of Greg.

Steve keeps torso-to-torso contact with Greg as shown and crawls up Greg's body. Steve has used his left hand to post under Greg's head for control.

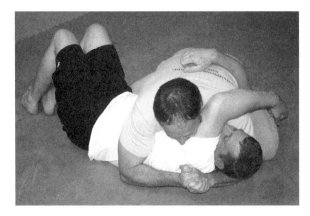

Steve crawls up Greg's body and finishes with a chest hold.

If Greg starts to escape, Steve might have to post his legs wide and arch his buttocks in this variation of the chest hold.

Steve has used his legs to sit through to provide a solid base to maintain control of Greg in this variation of the chest hold.

Both Legs Breakdown to Straddle Pin

Steve starts his both legs breakdown as described before.

Steve has broken Greg down and makes sure to keep a tight chest to torso contact with Greg.

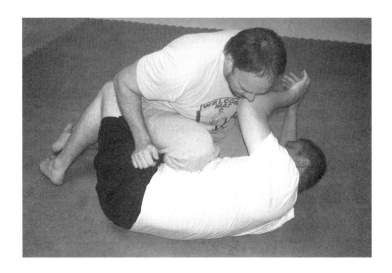

Steve quickly uses his right knee to "sneak" over Greg's hip to start the pin. Steve makes sure to jam his right knee firmly on Greg's gut as he gets it in position.

Steve uses his right arm to hook under Greg's far (right) leg as shown and uses his left hand to hook under Greg's head for maximum control. Steve is driving his right knee hard into Greg's stomach and torso (and ribcage). Steve is posting with his left leg for balance and support.

Front 2-Leg Breakdown to Chest Hold

Bill is on his elbows and knees in front of Eric.

Bill makes sure to jam his right shoulder into Eric's midsection before reaching out with both of his arms. After Bill gets good control with his right shoulder in Eric's gut, he grabs Eric's legs immediately above Eric's knees with both hands. Bill's knees are wide and his hips are low and feet digging into the mat for a good base.

Here's another view of how Bill sets up this breakdown. The left side of Bill's head is smashed against Eric's right hip for more control.

Bill uses his arms to scoop Eric's knees to Bill's right (and Eric's left) as Bill uses his head to drive into Eric's hip forcing Eric to tilt to Bill's right (and Eric's left).

Here's another view of how Bill tilts Eric to the right and uses his head to drive Eric in the direction Bill wants him to go.

Bill has scooped Eric's legs and broken him down onto his side. Notice bill's good lower body position, allowing Bill to move in for the pin.

Bill has moved to his right and up Eric's torso to apply the pin.

Bill finishes with a chest hold.

Bret is on top of Steve and Steve is on elbows and knees as shown. Steve positions his body so that his right shoulder is jammed into Bret's midsection and Steve's hips are moved to his right. Steve's head is near Bret's right hip at this point.

Steve firmly jams his right shoulder into Bret's midsection as he uses his right arm to grab around Bret's hip and back as shown. Steve uses his left hand to scoop or prop on the outside of Bret's right knee as shown.

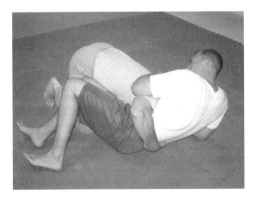

Steve drives hard into Bret with his right shoulder as he uses his left hand to scoop Bret's right knee. Steve has good control of Bret using his right arm and hand around Bret's waist. This action drives Bret to his right side as shown. Steve can immediately finish with a chest hold.

Here is a back view of how Steve has used his right arm to hook around Bret's left upper leg instead of grabbing around his waist. You may prefer to use this method of scooping both of your opponent's legs to break him down.

Steve is using his left hand to prop or scoop Bret's right knee and is using his right arm to hook and control Bret's left leg. Steve drives Bret to the mat in the direction of Bret's left side.

Steve has driven Bret to the mat and makes sure to drive his right shoulder hard into Bret's gut. Steve will move to his left and to Bret's side for the pin.

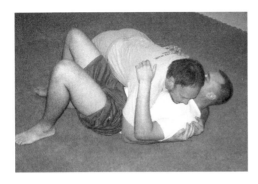

Steve finishes with a chest hold.

Judo/Sambo Switch

This is what I call a "get out of trouble move." It's a great move to put you in a better position or simply get out of a bad situation and end up in at least a neutral position. Eric is dominating Bill who is on the bottom on elbows and knees.

Bill makes sure to jam his left shoulder into Eric's midsection before he reaches with his hands. Notice that Bill has jammed his head on Eric's left hip. Bill has a solid base with knees wide, hips low and feet driving into the mat.

Bill uses the left side of his head to jam into Eric's left hip and uses both arms to scoop Eric's left leg immediately above the knee. Bill locks his hands together firmly. Bill is still on his knees but has started to move to his right and around Eric's left side.

Bill has turned the corner and moved around Eric's left side still keeping control with his head on Eric's left hip and grasping Eric's left leg with both of his hands and arms. Bill is still on his knees. I don't advocate doing a wrestler's sit-through when doing this move as it forces the attacker (in this case Bill) to shoot too far away from his opponent.

Bill continues to control Eric with his head on his left hip as he goes behind Eric. Bill uses his head to drive into Eric and force him to fall forward on his gut as shown.

Bill goes on top for a ride and can continue to control Eric by breaking him down further.

Sit-in to Guard from Wrestler's Ride

Jon is riding Travis and not letting Travis out of the bottom position.

Travis scoots his lower body out and away from Jon by moving his buttocks to Travis's right. As he does this, Travis uses his right hand to grab Jon's right wrist.

Travis continues to scoot his buttocks out and away from Jon as he pulls on Jon's right arm.

Travis starts his sit in by posting his left leg out as shown and makes sure to have the toes of his right foot digging into the mat. Travis keeps Jon's hand at his hip with his right hand.

Travis quickly swings his right foot into Jon and sits on his right buttocks as shown. Travis wants to jam his right foot under Jon's left leg to control him if he can.

Travis has done his sit in and had Jon in his guard.

Belt and Nelson to Chest Hold

This is a great breakdown my friend Bob Corwin teaches. This is a great breakdown for any sport that uses a jacket and belt. Steve is at Shawn's head on his knees with Shawn on elbows and knees as shown.

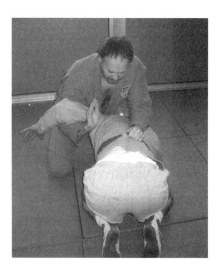

Steve positions his body so that it is immediately above Shawn's left shoulder. As he does this, Steve uses his left hand to grab Shawn's belt. Steve makes sure to place his left hand palm down and grab the belt. Steve's left forearm is driving on Shawn's spine. Steve uses his right arm to scoop under Shawn's left shoulder. Steve makes it a point to add more power to the move by pointing his right hand fingers to the ceiling.

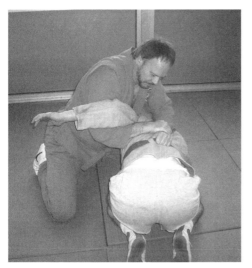

Steve moves to his right and starts to drive his torso under Shawn's left shoulder. This is an important point. If Steve doesn't do this, Shawn might be able to sit out and escape. Steve uses his right hand to grab his left wrist (and not Shawn's belt) for maximum control. Steve starts to drive Shawn to the mat.

Steve makes sure to never let go of Shawn's belt wit his left hand (so he can control him with the pin). Steve drives his chest up and under Shawn's left shoulder and drives Shawn over to his back.

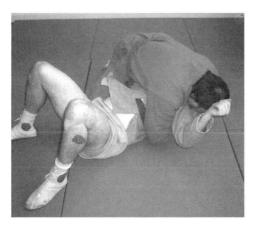

Steve finishes with a chest hold.

Belt and Nelson when Opponent is Flat

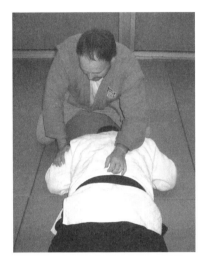

This is a variation of the belt and nelson when your opponent is flat on his face in the chicken position. Eric is on his face with Steve above him.

Steve uses both hands to scoop under Eric's left elbow. Notice how Steve is using his left elbow to wedge against Eric's spine. This is a bit painful to Eric and helps Steve lift the elbow better.

Steve uses his right arm to scoop under Eric's elbow as shown. Steve stays low and close to Eric for control.

Steve now uses his left hand to grab Eric's belt as shown as he uses his right arm to scoop and pull in tightly on Eric's left arm.

Steve uses his right hand to grab his left wrist as he continues to pull Eric's left arm tightly to his chest.

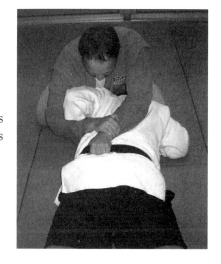

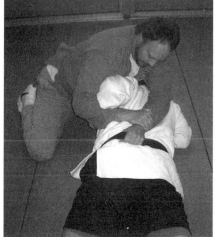

Steve moves to his right and uses his chest to drive up and under Eric's left shoulder.

Steve drives Eric over onto his back making sure to keep control of Eric's belt and arm scooped in tight.

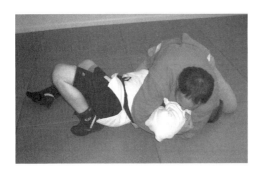

Steve finishes with a variation of the chest hold.

Bent Arm Breakdown to Chest Hold

Eric is in the chicken position and Steve is at the top.

Steve uses both of his arms and hands to scoop Eric's right elbow up. Steve is using his right elbow to wedge against Eric's spine for more cooperation from Eric.

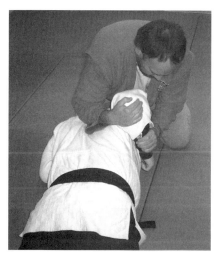

Steve uses his left hand to grab Eric's right wrist as he pulls up on Eric's right elbow with his right hand.

Steve keeps control with his left hand on Eric's wrist as he works his right hand over Eric's right upper arm. Steve is about to use his right hand to grab his left wrist.

Steve forms a figure four position with his hands and arms making sure to keep Eric's right wrist and hand close to Eric's body. Steve also starts to move to his left with his chest under Eric's right shoulder.

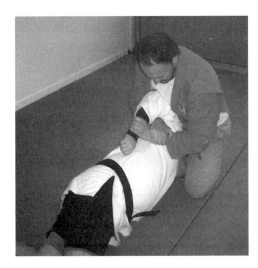

Steve uses both of his arms to pull Eric's shoulder close to Steve's chest and moves Eric onto his left side as shown. Notice that Steve is trapping Eric's head with his knees.

Steve moves to his left keeping control of Eric's right arm as he drives Eric over onto his back.

Steve can use his left hand and arm to scoop under Eric's right elbow, which makes this move work a bit better.

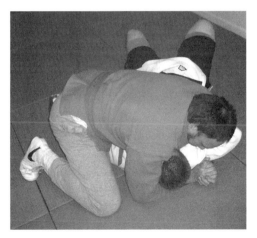

Steve finishes with a chest hold.

Bent Arm Breakdown to the German Pin

This is a slight variation of the bent arm breakdown, but it's finished with the German pin. Steve has started the bent arm breakdown on Greg and is using his right arm to jam hard into Greg's upper back as shown. Steve has his right knee jammed on the left side of Greg's head and has posted with his left leg.

Steve moves to his left and sucks Greg's right arm tight to his chest as shown. Steve is now crouched with his left leg in front of Greg's chest.

This photo is another view of how Steve has controlled Greg. Steve's right leg is now placed over Greg's head as shown.

Steve posts on his head as he rolls forward. As he does this, Steve uses his left leg to swing over Greg's body. Steve keeps firm control of Greg's arms.

Steve uses his left foot to drive under Greg's back. Steve is still posting on his head for control. Steve's right leg is trapping Greg's head.

Steve secures the hold and pins Greg with the German Pin. This is a cross between a chest hold and a vertical pin. It's not a common pin, but it does work. This pin works because Steve, on top, is basically sitting on Greg's right shoulder and has used his right leg to hook under Greg's head and left leg to hook under Greg's torso. Steve rests his body weight on Greg's shoulder as he controls Greg's right arm by either applying a bent armlock or even simply hugging it in tight. The reason this is called the "German" pin is because the first time I saw this, a German guy in a judo tournament somewhere in Europe did it back in the early 1980s.

The Power Half

This is a powerful move and even if you don't break your opponent down, you've given him a lot of grief for his troubles! Bryan is riding Drew and uses his left hand to hook under Drew's left shoulder and his right forearm to jam hard against Drew's neck and left shoulder as shown. Bryan grabs his hands together and forms a power half nelson.

Bryan moves to his left and drives hard onto Drew's neck with the half nelson. Bryan uses his left arm to lift up on Drew's left arm and shoulder as shown.

Bryan keeps moving to his left as he uses his half nelson to pry Drew over. Notice that Bryan keeps low with his head, not allowing Drew to sit in or escape. This also adds pressure to the half nelson.

This shows how Bryan is driving Drew over with the power half. Bryan keeps moving to his left, all the time prying Drew's shoulder up. There's a lot of pressure on the head and neck.

Bryan finishes with a chest hold.

Bar Arm and Shoulder Crank

When you use your forearm to jam against the back of your opponent's neck, this is a "bar arm." Think of your forearm as an iron bar. Bryan is applying a bar arm on Drew's neck from the top position with his right forearm.

Bryan keeps up the pressure with the bar arm wit his right arm as he uses his left hand to scoop Drew's right elbow out.

Bryan now uses his left hand to pull up on Drew's right elbow as Bryan moves to his left. Notice that Bryan is well balanced using his legs as a base. Bryan uses his right forearm to apply a lot of pressure on the back of Drew's neck at this point.

Bryan now has wrapped his left hand around Drew's right arm as shown and has used his right hand to pull Drew's right upper arm and shoulder close to his body. Bryan may have to lower his upper body to meet Drew's shoulder and arm. Bryan hugs Drew's right arm to his chest.

At this point, Bryan moves to this right around and behind Drew's body. Notice how Bryan hooks his left hand and arm under Drew's head, neck and right shoulder and Bryan has used his right hand to reach under Drew's body at the hips to help control him further.

As Bryan moves to his right, he hooks his left arm under Drew's head and neck controlling the upper body. Bryan uses his head on Drew's chest for control and has reached his right arm and hand under Drew's back at the hips to control Drew, with a variation of the chest hold.

Over and Under Breakdown

Steve is at Greg's head with Greg on his elbows and knees. Steve uses his right arm to hook under Greg's left shoulder. Steve makes sure to keep his chest close on Greg's upper back.

Steve moves his lower body to his right (toward Greg's left hip) and as he does this, uses his left hand to scoop Greg's right elbow. Steve uses his right hand to continue to hook under Greg's left shoulder. This action starts to force Greg to roll over his left shoulder.

Steve has rolled Greg over onto his back and finishes with a chest hold.

Heckadon Over and Under

This is a variation of the over and under that World Sambo Champion Chris Heckadon used. Steve uses his right arm to hook under Greg's left shoulder as he uses his left hand to scoop Greg's right arm. Steve has moved his body to his left and is on his knees.

Steve uses his left hand to scoop on Greg's right elbow as he uses his right hand to reach over Greg's back and lock onto Greg's right hip trapping Greg's left arm as shown. Steve is driving hard into Greg and has his upper chest immediately under Greg's left shoulder.

Steve has turned Greg over and finishes with a chest hold.

Near Leg Roll to Scarf Hold

Steve controls Eric with a near leg ride as shown.

Steve continues to control Eric with the near leg ride as he uses his right arm to hook over Eric's right shoulder and upper arm.

Steve uses his right arm and hand to grab around Eric's waist. Steve wants to use his left hand to grab Eric's left jacket lapel if he can. If he can, Steve can use his left hand to hook under Eric's left armpit.

Steve has now controlled Eric's upper body and continues to use the near leg ride. Steve uses his right foot to hook into his leg forming a triangle with his legs on Eric's right leg.

Steve rolls to his back as he pulls Eric over with him. Steve must explode into this breakdown. This is done best if it's done in an explosive movement rather than a slow, gradual roll.

Steve has rolled Eric over and continues on to the scarf hold or chest hold.

Near Wrist and Tilt

Bryan is riding Drew and has used his left hand to grab Drew's left wrist.

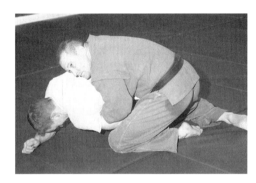

Bryan sucks Drew's left wrist into Drew's body as shown.

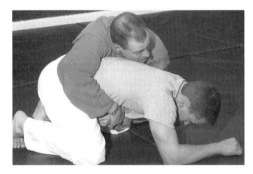

To control Drew's body, Bryan is using his right arm to reach around Drew's right hip and has grabbed Drew's left wrist with both of his hands.

This shows how Bryan has used both of his arms to grab Drew's left forearm and wrist. This is a great way to control your opponent when riding him from the top, but it helps Bryan cinch Drew's arm to his body and limits his ability to get away.

Bryan uses his right hand to start to reach behind Drew as shown. Bryan wants to use his right hand to reach through Drew's legs.

Bryan has used his right hand to reach between Drew's legs and has grabbed Drew's left wrist as shown. Bryan uses his right hand to pull hard forcing Drew to tilt onto his left shoulder.

As he uses his right hand to pull on Drew's left wrist, Bryan moves to his left and around Drew's back as shown. Bryan uses his left hand to push on Drew's left shoulder and upper back.

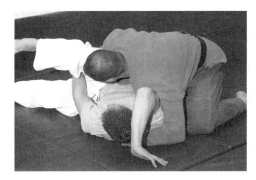

Bryan has now moved to his left and keeps control with his right hand on Drew's left wrist puling it hard. Dong this pulls Drew's left arm into his crotch. Bryan uses his left hand and arm to scoop under Drew's shoulder and neck.

Bryan finishes with a chest hold.

The Judo/Sambo Stack

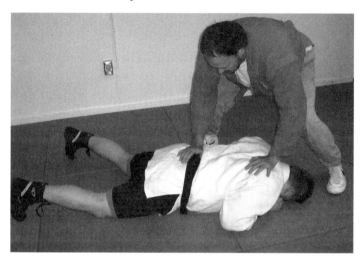

This is an explosive and effective move when your opponent is face down on the mat.

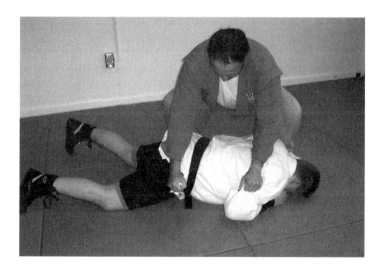

Steve moves to Eric's left side and squats as shown. Steve uses both hands to grab the far side of Eric's body. Steve's left hand is at Eric's triceps and Steve's right hand is grabbing Eric's jacket near the hip. Eric is in sambo gear and doesn't have pants for Steve to grab with his right hand.

This shows Steve using his right hand to grab Greg's pants immediately above the right knee. This grip is powerful because Steve has control of Greg's upper body and lower body as well.

Steve stays in the squatting position and jumps back, making sure not to fall on his buttocks. As he does this, Steve pulls hard with both hands on Greg's jacket and pants pulling Greg onto his back.

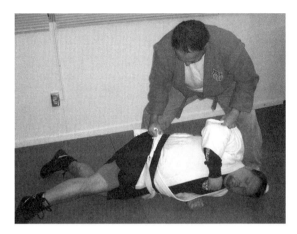

This shows how Steve has jumped back and is pulling Eric in a sambo uniform. Instead of using his right hand to grab the pants, Steve is using it to grab the lower part of the jacket.

Steve jumps back in an explosive action and pulls Eric hard onto his back. Steve makes sure to keep firm control with both hands and plants Eric hard onto his back.

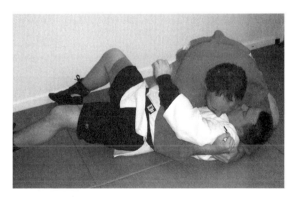

Steve finishes with a chest hold.

Burns Breakdown (Both Lapels) to Upper Chest Hold

This series of breakdowns is named after AnnMaria (Burns) Demars, the first American to win a world judo championship (in 1984). She was the first to show it to me back in the 1970s and it's worked well ever since.

Eric is flat on his stomach with Steve riding him. Steve has his left knee on the mat and his right leg posted as shown.

Steve reaches with both hands under Eric's armpits and grabs his lapels.

Steve quickly hops to his left (to Eric's right) and stays on both knees.

Steve quickly hops to his left (to Eric's right) over Eric's back making sure to stay on his knees and even on a foot, but definitely not fall on his side or buttocks. As Steve does this, he jerks hard on Eric's lapels as shown.

Steve pulls Eric back using his strong lapel grip and the weight of his body. If necessary (and I recommended it) Steve jams his chin down hard on Eric's left collarbone and shoulder and uses his head to push Eric's body down onto the mat.

This closer view shows you how using your chin on your opponent's shoulder and collarbone helps pull him in tighter and onto the mat. Steve is holding Eric's lapels tightly and using his hands to pull Eric down as well.

Steve finishes the breakdown and settles in for an upper body hold as shown. Notice that Eric's head is jammed forward with Steve's right shoulder directly behind it. If Steve is applying too much pressure (a neck crank) and the rules of the sport don't allow for it, he can ease off the neck pressure.

Burns Breakdown (Both Wrists)

This is the same Burns Breakdown only this time Steve is behind Ed as shown and is using both of his hands to grab both of Ed's wrists. Steve is at Ed's left side.

Here's another view of the starting position of this breakdown.

Notice how Steve has grasped Ed's wrists and not wrapped his thumb over Ed's wrists. This is called a "meat hook" grip and works well in this situation. This gives Steve better control and flexibility. Steve is pulling Ed's wrists in tight to his body.

Steve has quickly jumped to the opposite side of Ed and has stayed on his knees and feet as shown. If you fall on your side or roll over onto your buttocks and back, you lose a lot of the control and explosive power that make this move work.

Steve is using his chin on Ed's collarbone to help pull him down onto the mat. Notice the control of both of Ed's wrists.

Steve pulls Ed down onto his back and pulls down hard with both hands on Ed's wrists to control them better. Steve finishes with an upper chest hold.

Burns Breakdown (Wrist and Lapel)

This variation of the breakdown uses both the lapel and wrist of your opponent.

Steve is at Eric's left side on his knees. He uses his left hand to grab Eric's left lapel and his right hand to grab Eric's right wrist.

Steve quickly jumps to the other side of Eric's body as shown.

Steve uses his left hand on Eric's lapel to pull him over along with his right hand on Eric's right wrist as shown. Steve uses his chin to jam into Eric's collarbone and shoulder to drive him down to the mat.

Here's another view of how Steve is positioned behind Eric as he pulls him to the mat.

Steve keeps hold of both the lapel and wrist and settles into an upper chest pin.

Usually, Steve will have to release Eric's wrist and grab his lapel as shown to secure the pin.

Triangle Breakdown from Top to Triangle Pin

Kirk in at the top of Travis who is on his elbows and knees as shown. Kirk uses his right leg to dig under Travis' left armpit. Kirk makes sure to have his left knee jammed hard on Travis's shoulder.

Kirk uses his right hand to grab Travis's belt and uses his left hand to grab Travis' right sleeve.

Kirk rolls to his left as shown and will roll Travis over with him.

Kirk ends up in the position shown and uses his left hand to pull on Travis's left wrist or arm to tighten the hold. Kirk forms a triangle with his legs, making sure the top leg (here, Kirk's left leg) scoops under Travis's left upper arm. The top of Kirk's left foot goes into the back on his right knee to form the triangle.

Kirk uses his right hand to scoop under Travis's right arm for control of it. Notice that Kirk is on his side.

Kirk uses his left hand now to grab Travis's pants so Kirk can pull himself on top of Travis.

119

Kirk is now on top of Travis and switches the way his legs are crossed for more control. Kirk has used his left hand to reach on the inside of Travis's right leg and grabs it.

Kirk has switched the way his legs are crossed for more control and finishes with the triangle pin.

Here's another view of the triangle pin.

Triangle Front Roll from the Top to Triangle Pin

Bill is standing in front of Steve who is on his knees.

Bill uses his left leg to step over Steve's right shoulder.

Bill quickly uses his right leg to swing under Steve's neck as shown. Bill will have to use his right hand to post to the side for stability.

Bill continues to jam his right leg under Steve's head and chest as he falls onto his right side. Bill makes sure to uses his right foot to scoop up under Steve's right armpit as shown.

Bill uses the top of his right foot to lock in the back of his left knee and this action squeezes Steve's upper body hard. As he does this, Bill uses his left hand to grab Steve's pants (and belt if he had one). Bill starts to shift his body weight and momentum back toward his buttocks.

Bill pulls Steve over as he rolls over his buttocks.

Bill rolls Steve over his head and onto his back. Bill cinches in the triangle he has formed with his legs and uses his right hand to grab inside Steve's left legs as shown to secure the triangle pin.

Top Triangle Double Trouble from Mount

Travis is on Jon in the mount position.

Travis uses his right hand to scoop under Jon's head as he uses his left hand to post above Jon for stability.

Travis uses his right hand to pull up on Jon's head and moves his right knee forward under Jon's left arm and shoulder. Travis uses his left hand to pull Jon's right arm down.

Travis lets go of Jon's arm and uses his left foot and leg to step over it.

Travis uses his left leg to hook under Jon's head and neck. Travis uses his left hand to post for stability and places his weight on his left knee after he sinks it in place.

Travis leans to his left and forms a triangle with his legs trapping Jon's head, left arm and left shoulder.

Travis leans back and sits on Jon as shown securing the triangle pin. As in all triangle pins, you can choke your opponent as well as pin him, so this is double trouble for him!

In MMA or in a real fight, Travis can use this position to punch Jon.

Rolling Banana Split to the Upper Back Pin

This pin is a variation of the old judo hold-down, ura gatame, or upper back pin. Bret is using a near leg ride on Eric as shown.

Bret has used his right leg to lace around Eric's right leg and is using his left hand to grab Eric's right ankle.

Here's another view of Bret riding Eric and using his left hand to grab Eric's left ankle. At this point, Bret turns his body to face backward on Eric.

Bret uses his left hand to anchor Eric's left ankle as he uses his right arm to reach in over Eric's left hip as shown. Bret is curling up and leaning over Eric's body as shown.

Bret starts to roll over his right shoulder and over Eric's lower back and hips as he uses both hands to scoop Eric's left ankle.

Bret has rolled over Eric's body using both hands to hold onto Eric's left ankle. As he does this, Bret uses his right leg to hook over Eric's right leg as shown.

Bret secures the upper back pin and forms a triangle on Eric's right leg. Bret "splits" Eric apart at this point and this can also be used as a hip joint lock.

Sit-back Banana Split to the Upper Back Pin

This variation of the banana split doesn't require Bret to roll over Eric. Bret has Eric in a near leg ride.

Bret uses his left hand and arm to reach behind Eric's left buttocks. Bret uses his left hand to scoop up and under Eric's left knee as shown.

Bret grabs his hands together as shown and leans back. As he does this, he pulls Eric back with him. Notice that Bret's left leg is still laced around Eric's right leg.

A Bret rolls back pulling Eric with him and as he does, splits Eric apart to secure the upper back pin.

The Gut Wrench to the Hip Hold

I remember watching Greg Gibson, the first American to win a World Sambo Championship, use this move at the Sambo Nationals. His gut wrench really lived up to its name; it was put on so hard and Gibson squeezed so much that his opponents seemingly were willing to roll onto their back and let him hold them.

Steve is riding John in this photo.

Steve uses his right arm to reach around John's hips and lower back and grabs both of his hands together. Steve squeezes as hard as possible and makes this uncomfortable for John. Steve uses his head to jam on John's left hip. This controls John well.

Continuing to squeeze John's midsection hard, Steve uses his head to drive hard into the "hole" created by John's position on elbows and knees on the mat.

Steve drives his head into the hole and starts to pull John over as he rolls.

Steve rolls John over onto his back.

Note the continued gut wrench action of the arms as Steve controls John's body. Steve keeps his head tight against John's left hip as he completes the roll.

Steve rolls over on top of John and secures the hip hold.

The Polish Whizzer to the Upper Chest Pin

Steve is at Eric's head and Eric is on elbows and knees. Steve is positioned slightly above Eric's right shoulder.

Steve uses his right hand to grab Eric's left lapel.

Steve uses his left hand to scoop Eric's right elbow and pull it out giving himself room to work.

Steve uses his left hand to scoop under Eric's left upper arm (not tight and in close under the shoulder as this would give Steve no room to work). Steve places the back of his left hand and on the back of Eric's head.

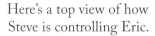

Here's a top view of how Steve is controlling Eric.

Steve quickly rolls over his left shoulder as shown, making sure to keep pulling with his right hand on Eric's lapel. Steve rolls his head through the hole Eric created by being on all fours.

Steve rolls hard pulling Eric over with him. Notice how Steve is using his left hand on the back of Eric's head for shoulder, head and neck control.

Steve rolls Eric over onto his back.

Steve finishes with a variation of the chest hold. At no point does Steve ever let go of Eric's lapel wit his right hand. Notice how Steve's left arm is wedged under Eric's head and grabbing his left shoulder for better control.

Steve can lean back and extend his legs as shown for more control if needed.

Another variation of this pin is for Steve to sit through with his right leg as shown.

Peterson Roll to Rear Scarf Hold and Vertical Hold

Travis is riding Vince from the side and has used his right hand to reach far around Vince's hip.

Vince uses his right hand to grab Travis's right wrist. As he does this, Vince scoots his buttocks out to his right.

Vince rolls Travis over as shown.

Vince uses his left leg to spring Travis over as they roll. This "leg assist" helps in rolling Travis over. Vince continues to hold tight with his right hand on Travis's right wrist.

Vince has rolled Travis over his back and rolled on top of him. Vince has continued to use his right hand to hold onto Travis's right wrist and now pulls it tightly around his back causing a lot of pressure on Travis's ribs and torso.

Here's another view of how Vince rolled Travis over. Vince is using his left hand to grab Travis's belt for more control. Notice Vince's good base with his legs. If Vince chooses, he can pin Travis with this variation of the rear scarf hold.

Vince wants to pin Travis with a vertical hold or even control him with a mount, so Vince uses his right arm and hand to reach over Travis as shown.

Vince uses his right hand to scoop Travis's left leg immediately above the knee as shown. Vince uses his right hand to pull Travis's left leg in.

Vince uses his right hand to pull in on Travis's left knee as he swings his right leg over.

Vince swings his leg over and gets on top of Travis.

Vince has secured the vertical pin and is using a grapevine variation to control Travis's legs and lower body for more control.

Soden Roll to Scarf Hold

This breakdown is named after Steve Soden, a Welcome Mat athlete who used is with great success in his career.

Shawn is on elbows and knees with Steve above him.

Shawn traps both of Steve's arms with his own arms as shown and pulls Steve on him. As he does this, Shawn quickly uses his right leg to sit through in an explosive movement.

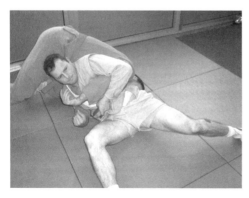

As Shawn sits through, he keeps firm control of both of Steve's arms and rolls Steve over.

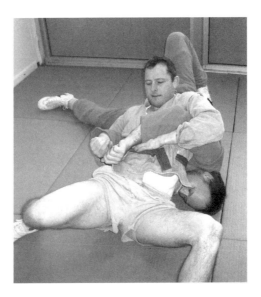

Shawn rolls Steve over onto his back and makes sure his left hip is near Steve's head.

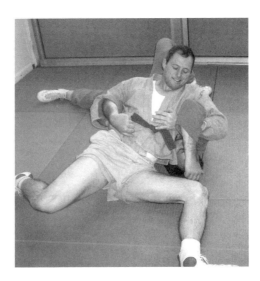

Shawn keeps control with both hands as shown, pulling hard on both of Steve's arms. Shawn sits through into a variation of the scarf hold, keeping his left hip near Steve's head.

Hip Wheel Breakdown to Scarf Hold

Josh and Chance are both on their knees. Josh uses his right hand to grab around Chance's head as he uses his left hand to pull on Chance's right sleeve.

Josh turns his right hip into Chance and continues his strong pull with his left hand on chance's sleeve. Josh will basically do a hip wheel throw while on the knees and roll Chance over his right hip.

Josh immediately secures a scarf hold after rolling Chance over.

Hip Shift to Upper Chest Hold

Steve is using a rodeo ride to control Bret. Steve is using both hands to grab Bret's lapels.

Steve rolls Bret over and both are seated on their buttocks. Steve keeps good control with his legs as shown and continues to hold both lapels.

Steve drops his left leg behind Bret and uses his right foot to hook under Bret's right knee as shown.

Here's another view of how Steve positions himself behind Bret. Steve scoots back a bit with his buttocks and gives himself a bit more room between his body and Bret's body.

Steve rolls to his left hip and uses his right leg and foot to kicks Bret's right leg over as shown. This action rolls Bret over to his left hip and side.

Steve has continued to keep control of Bret's lapels with both of his hands and puts Bret on his back as shown.

Steve settles in with an upper chest pin continuing to hold both of Bret's lapels.

Steve can sit through if necessary in this variation of the upper chest hold.

Russian Roll to Chest Hold

Bryan is riding Drew from the side as shown.

Bryan uses his right hand to reach under Jarrod's left armpit and grab Jarrod's far (right) lapel. Notice that Bryan is positioned higher on Jarrod and has the right side of his head on Jarrod's back.

Bryan uses his left hand to grab inside Jarrod's collar.

Bryan rolls backward toward Jarrod's feet as he pulls with both hands.

Bryan rolls hard down the back of Jarrod continuing to pulls with both hands. This forces Jarrod to rise up and roll to his back as shown.

Bryan completes the roll and puts Jarrod onto his back.

Bryan rolls over on top of Jarrod and puts his head on Jarrod's chest to control him. Bryan will finish with a chest hold.

Breakdowns When One Opponent is Standing and the Other is Kneeling

One grappler standing and the other kneeling is a common situation in all combat sports and fighting circumstances. These moves are sometimes called "transitions" because they link groundfighting to fighting from a standing position. But, like all breakdowns, these skills take an opponent from a stable to an unstable position and are vital for every grappler to know. I've classified this position into 2 major groups.

1. **Bottom to Top Position:** when you are on the bottom and have to get up or break your opponent down to the mat to continue on to groundfighting.

2. **Top to Bottom Position:** when you are standing and your opponent is on his knees and you want to break him down to engage him in groundfighting.

I honestly haven't seen many books cover on this phase of grappling and it's hoped that this look at these valuable breakdowns will be of help. Also, knowing how to get up if you are the guy stuck on the bottom is pretty useful and will get you out of trouble when you're in this position. Several moves from each position are presented.

Get Up from the Bottom Position

This is a good way to get to a standing position if your opponent has knocked you down.

Bryan is on his knees with Trevor dominating him as shown. Bryan makes sure to uses his left hand to grab Trevor's right lapel.

Bryan keeps hold using his left hand on Trevor's lapel as Bryan uses his right hand to post on the mat. Notice that Bryan is low with his knees wide and toes digging into the mat for stability.

Bryan continues to post with his right hand for support as he squats back keeping his weight in his buttocks and keeping his hips away from Trevor. If Bryan is too close to Trevor or comes up on one knee, Trevor will easily throw him or break him down.

Bryan continues to back out and away from Trevor and is on his feet.

Top to Bottom Inner Thigh Throw

What Bryan doesn't want to do is try to get up like this. If he steps up with one knee up, he's vulnerable to Trevor dominating him and taking him back down to the mat. In a judo or sambo match, Trevor will score big points by slamming Bryan to the mat with a throw from this position!

Trevor uses his left hand to grab Bryan's sleeve and uses his right hand to grab Bryan's collar. Trevor turns in and will use his right leg to sweep Bryan's left (supporting) leg.

Trevor uses his right leg to sweep Bryan's left leg in an uchi mata (inner thigh) throw.

Trevor throws Bryan to the mat and will follow through with a pin or submission technique.

Top to Bottom Outside Leg Hook

Bryan tries to get up on one knee and this time Trevor will reverse directions and use a leg hook to take Bryan onto his back.

Trevor keeps hold with his left hand on Bryan's right sleeve and right hand on Bryan's collar as he turns around toward Bryan. Trevor uses his left hand on Bryan's sleeve to pull Bryan's right arm.

Trevor keeps turning and uses his left leg to hook Bryan's left leg as shown.

This hooking action and Trevor's body driving forward throws Bryan with an o soto gari (major outer reap) throw.

Trevor throws Bryan to the mat and will follow through with a pin or submission technique.

Spin and Pin

Bryan is standing and Trevor is on his knees as shown. Bryan is using his right hand to grab Trevor's jacket between the shoulder blades. Bryan is using his left hand to control Trevor's right sleeve.

Bryan steps forward with his right foot and leg and places his right heel on the outside of Trevor's right knee. As he does this, Bryan pulls Trevor into him as shown. Bryan will spin and take Trevor directly to Trevor's right side and not forward.

Bryan spins Trevor to the mat as shown.

Bryan lands on Trevor and pins him with a scarf hold.

Snap Down and Go Behind

Bryan is standing and Trevor is on his knees. Bryan scoots back a bit creating space between the two bodies. Bryan is using his right hand high on Trevor's back grabbing between the shoulder blades.

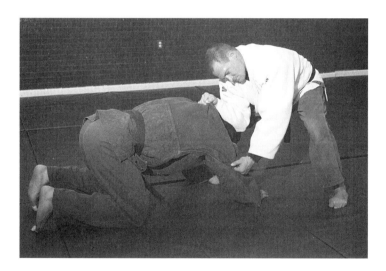

Bryan snaps Trevor down to the mat forward as shown.

Bryan has snapped Trevor down to his hands and knees and goes behind for a ride.

Bryan secures the wrestler's ride and will go for further control from here.

Snap Down to Belt and Nelson

Bryan is standing and Drew is on his knees. Bryan has control of Drew's upper back with a strong jacket grip between the shoulder blades as shown.

Bryan snaps Drew forward and down to the mat keeping control with his right hand on Drew's jacket.

Bryan uses his left hand to scoop under Drew's right shoulder and upper arm as shown. Bryan has now also used his right hand to reach down and grab Drew's belt (palm down).

Bryan quickly moves to his left and up and under Drew's right shoulder using his left hand to scoop under Drew's arm and shoulder. Bryan keeps control of Drew's belt with his right hand. Bryan will use his left hand to grab his right wrist for more control as he starts the breakdown.

Bryan drives Drew over, making sure to stay low and under Drew's right shoulder to keep Drew from sitting out and out of trouble.

Bryan drives Drew to the mat and finishes with a chest hold.

Top to Bottom Shoulder Lock Scissors Pin

Steve is on his knees and Bill is standing. Bill moves to Steve's right side and uses his right arm to reach under Steve's right arm and shoulder. Bill uses his left hand to reach over the top of Steve's right shoulder. Bill grabs his hands together and squeezes Steve tight.

Bill quickly moves to his left and behind Steve. Bill keeps his head planted on Steve's right shoulder as shown.

Bill uses his left leg to hook under Steve's body as Bill drives forward over Steve's body.

Bill drives Steve over, all the while keeping control with his hands and arms around Steve's head and shoulder. Bill finishes the pin by hooking his ankles together to keep Steve from moving. This pin is a variation of the shoulder lock.

Top to Bottom Hug and Hold

Bryan is standing and Drew is on his knees. Bryan has control of Drew with a high back jacket grip with his right hand and a sleeve grip with his left hand.

Bryan turns in toward Drew and uses his left arm to scoop under Drew's right armpit. As he does this, Bryan uses his right hand and arm to reach around and grab his left hand, locking them tightly. Bryan shoots his hips back and away from Drew for more control.

Bryan quickly turns to his right and spins Drew to the mat in a bear hug.

Bryan finishes with a chest hold.

Bottom to Top Double Leg Breakdown

Drew is on his knees with Bryan standing.

Drew moves in quickly on his knees as shown and uses his right hand to grab around Bryan's left hip. Drew makes sure his right shoulder is in tight against Bryan's midsection. The right side of Drew's head is on Bryan's right hip.

Here's another view of how Drew gets close in to take Bryan to the mat. Notice that Drew hasn't grabbed his hands together and is using his hands to hook hard immediately above Bryan's knees.

Drew scoops his hands and drive Bryan onto his back.

Drew had taken Bryan to the mat and is in between his legs. Drew has broken Bryan down into a neutral position and is no longer being dominated by Bryan.

Bottom to Top Double Leg Inside Hook Breakdown

Alan is on his knees with Kyle standing above him.

Alan uses his right leg to hook inside of Kyle's right ankle as shown. Alan is using his left hand to grab Kyle's right leg and has his head on the outside of Kyle's right knee.

Alan uses both hands to grab Kyle's legs immediately above Kyle's knees and starts to tackle Kyle.

Here's another view of how Alan is starting to tackle Kyle.

Alan scoops hard with both arms and drives his body into Kyle taking him to the mat.

Alan has taken Kyle to the mat and continues to hold onto both of Kyle's legs with his arms and hugs tightly using his head.

Alan moves to his left and around Kyle's body and uses a chest hold.

Bottom to Top Leg Scoop

Bryan is on his knees with Drew standing. Bryan makes sure to use his right hand to control Drew's left lapel and collar. Bryan is using his left hand to grab Drew's right sleeve.

Bryan uses his right leg to step in deep between Drew's legs and plants the right side of his head on Drew's right hip. Bryan still has control with his right hand of Drew's collar. Bryan uses his right hand to grab Drew's right ankle (palm up) as shown.

Bryan pulls hard with his right hand on Drew's collar as he uses his left hand to scoop upward on Drew's right ankle. Bryan leans toward his right rear as he does this but maintains his balance on his foot and knee as shown.

Bryan uses his head to drive into Drew toward Bryan's right rear side as he continues to pull with his right hand on Drew's collar. Bryan continues to use his left hand to lift Drew's right foot as shown. Bryan explodes to his feet as he does this.

Bryan continues to pull on Drew's collar with his right hand and he continues his lifting of Drew's right ankle with his left hand as shown.

Bryan slams Drew back down onto his back onto the mat and will finish him with a chest hold.

Bottom to Top 2-on-1 Breakdown

Alan is on his knees with Kyle standing.

Alan steps deep between Kyle's legs with his right foot and places the right side of his head on Kyle's right hip.

Alan uses his right leg to hook Kyle's right ankle and as he does, Alan uses his left arm to reach around Kyle's right leg and uses his left hand to grab Kyle's left wrist. Alan then uses both hands to grab Kyle's left wrist as shown. This traps Kyle momentarily.

176

Alan uses his right hand to hook around Kyle's left leg immediately below the knee and starts the breakdown. Alan will drive hard into Kyle and take him to the mat.

Alan has taken Kyle to the mat onto his back.

Alan quickly moves to his left and secures a scarf hold.

Bottom to Top Knee Trap Inside Leg Hook

Kyle is standing with Alan on his knees.

Alan closes the space between himself and Kyle leading with his right hip. As he does this, Alan moves his right knee behind Kyle's right ankle as shown. Alan uses his left hand to grab Kyle's right wrist or forearm.

Alan uses his right knee to trap Kyle's right ankle and lower leg.

Alan quickly uses his right hand to scoop around Kyle's left leg as shown. Alan drives Kyle to the mat trapping his right ankle and leg.

Alan takes Kyle to the mat.

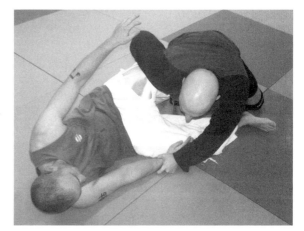

Alan moves around Kyle to his left and goes for a pin.

Bottom to Top Double Ankle Hook

My wife Becky used this breakdown with success during her career. Bryan is on his knees with Trevor standing. Bryan is using his right hand to hold Trevor's left lapel and is using his left hand to hold Trevor's right sleeve.

Bryan uses his left hand to support himself as he sits in and under Trevor. Bryan is sitting on his buttocks and continues to use his right hand to hold Trevor's lapel.

Bryan quickly uses his left hand to again grab Trevor's right sleeve and uses both feet to hook behind Trevor's ankles as shown.

Bryan pushes on Trevor with his hand and arms and uses the weight of his body to drive forward, all the while using both feet to hook Trevor's ankles.

Bryan pushes Trevor back onto the mat.

Bryan ends up on top of Trevor and moves around his body for a chest hold.

Bottom to Top Double Leg Trap to Chest Hold

Bryan is on his knees with Trevor standing. Bryan uses his right hand to hold onto Trevor's left lapel. Bryan uses his left hand to post onto the mat.

Bryan uses his left leg to sit into Trevor as shown.

Bryan keeps control with his right hand on Trevor's lapel and jams his right foot into Trevor's midsection.

Bryan rolls into Trevor on his left side and uses his left hand to scoop under Trevor's right leg as shown. Bryan's right foot is jammed in Trevor's midsection with Bryan's toes pointed in and heel out.

Bryan now drives his right leg between Trevor's legs and hooks Trevor's left leg. Bryan uses his left arm and hand to hook behind Trevor's right ankle and lower leg.

Bryan hooks Trevor with his arm and leg and takes him to the mat.

Bryan follows up with a chest hold.

Bottom to Top Double Leg Trap Roll

This is a variation of the double leg trap. Bryan has worked his body into the position shown here.

Bryan pulls Trevor forward with his right hand on the lapel and keeps his right foot jammed in Trevor's midsection.

Bryan rolls Trevor forward and uses his left hand to hook Trevor's right leg for more control.

Bryan rolls Trevor over and will go on top of him for a pin.

Bottom to Top Double Leg Circle Throw to Vertical Pin

Bryan is on both knees with Trevor standing.

Bryan quickly gets to a squatting position and keeps hold of Trevor with his right hand on the lapel. Bryan uses his left hand to post onto the mat for stability.

Bryan swings his body in tightly and deeply under Trevor's body and places both of his feet on Trevor's hips, making sure the toes are pointed outward.

Bryan rolls Trevor over with both legs on both hips.

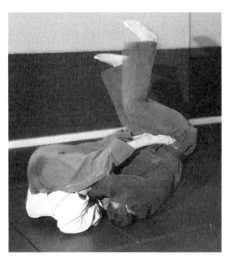

Bryan does a backward somersault and continues to roll Trevor over with a tomoe nage (circle throw).

Bryan rolls over on top of Trevor and finishes with a vertical pin.

SECTION FOUR:
The Guard Position

"Get your opponent at a disadvantage, and never, on any account,
fight him on equal terms."

~ George Bernard Shaw

What came to be known as the "guard" position in the early 1990s is old-school groundfighting from the early days of judo and credit should be given to the Brazilian jiujitsu exponents for revitalizing this great fighting position. I remember learning this position as a young kid when I started judo in the 1960s. This position obviously dates back much farther than that, going back to the 1880s when Prof. Jigoro Kano developed Kodokan Judo in Japan. This position has been known by various names through the years and calling it the guard describes it well. Wrestlers from western traditions such as freestyle, collegiate and folkstyle have a tough time with grapplers who use the guard. In western wrestling, athletes are taught that if they are on their backs, they're losing. In the Japanese tradition of grappling, fighting off your back, buttocks or hips is simply another way of gaining an advantage.

There have been quite a few good books written that concentrate primarily on the guard position, so if you're a person who focuses his efforts mostly on this position in grappling, and while this book deals with a broad range of breaking an opponent down, I hope the skills presented here add to the body of knowledge in a positive way. What I've included in this section are skills that have worked well for my athletes and me as well as what I've observed others doing at elite levels of competition and training in judo, sport jujitsu and submission grappling.

The guard is one of many good positions that are used and have stood the test of both time and competition. From my perspective in judo, sambo, sport jujitsu and submission grappling, as well as mixed martial arts, a fighter has to be well rounded and have several specific skills from a variety of positions. If he concentrates too heavily on only one position or aspect of fighting or grappling, he will quickly run out of ideas and get beat by someone who is better trained in more phases and aspects of grappling or fighting. If you concentrate too much on fighting from only one position, you are (literally and figuratively) one dimensional as a grappler and will be defeated. Take the time and effort to learn how to fight from a variety of positions and as you improve, you will be able to dictate what position will develop in an actual fight or match.

You can't impose your will on your opponent until you are able to adapt to a variety of situations that come up in a real match or fight. Remember that one of the most important components in success in grappling is mobility. No matter what position you fight from or find yourself in, you must have the ability to move and dictate the movement of your opponent. Remember this when fighting from the guard and make a real effort to avoid laying flat on your back, which often prohibits you from good mobility. Try to fight from your buttocks and off your hip so you can maneuver both your own body and limbs and your opponent's body and limbs. However, having said that, there are times you may have an advantage if you are flat on your back. A good example is when you have your opponent in your closed guard and are setting him up for another move. In some cases, you may have to lie flat on your back when you manipulate your opponent's legs or hips. Position is such a fluid thing that there are often no absolute rules that apply to everything, but there are general rules (as we have been discussing) that serve your purposes well.

Basically, there are two primary ways of fighting from the guard position. You are either in an "open" guard, where you are using your feet and legs to manipulate your opponent and haven't wrapped them around his body and pulled him to you. When you wrap your legs around your opponent's body and hook your ankles or legs together that is the "closed" guard. These positions will be discussed a bit later.

When you are in your opponent's guard, you will usually be kneeling or standing. Knowing how to intelligently fight someone while you are in his guard is important, and the best advice I give to athletes is, "Patience is a virtue." If you are in your opponent's guard, don't get too anxious or impatient in an attempt to get past his legs or work a move on him. Take your time, work logically from one thing to the next and make sure you use small movements rather than large, reaching or sweeping movements. When you are in an opponent's guard, stay below his belt line or hip line. I call this "staying south of the border." If you reach past his belt or hips, you are over-reaching and extending yourself too far forward and he will take advantage of your weak position. Too many novices try to secure a scoring move or submission before securing or nullifying an opponent's lower body when they are in someone's guard. I'll discuss this a bit more later.

Some terms that are used in this book may differ slightly with some of the nomenclature currently in use, but these are terms I've used for some time and describe the actions in a similar way. I use the word "rollover" to describe what has come to be known as a "sweep." Call it what you want, it's the same thing. "Passing the guard" or "passing by the opponent's legs" simply means getting past your opponent's leg or legs to apply a move. "Shrimping" is when you curl up tightly onto one hip. This creates a smaller area where your opponent can attack you from and is an excellent way of moving on the mat if you are in the bottom position.

Groundfighting in the Guard Position

It's important when you are in the guard position that you protect your middle. In this photo, Bret is shrimped on his side and keeping Steve away by using his feet and hands. If Steve gets past Bret's feet, knees, legs, hands and arms (in other words, Bret's "guard") he can establish a better position or pin Bret. When fighting from the guard position, the bottom grappler should be curled up like a shrimp and fight off his buttocks or hips. I rarely advocate fighting from flat off your back. If you're flat on your back, you lose a great deal of mobility, and mobility and movement are essential to fighting well from the guard position. Bret is fighting from an "open guard." This means he is using his feet to try to control Steve's movements and hasn't pulled Steve in tight to his body and crossed his ankles or legs.

Stay South of the Border

If you're the top grappler between your opponent's legs, make sure you stay below his belt or hip line and take your time. Don't rush in and over-extend yourself. Be patient, stay compact and don't hook your arm under your opponent's leg. If you do this, he can work his leg over your shoulder and get you in a triangle choke. Keep your hands and elbows in close and wedged in your opponent's upper legs and thighs for control. A lot of grapplers get caught up in the emotion of the fight and think they have to rush things. Take your time, be patient and pick your shots. Stay compact and don't give the bottom grappler a chance to manipulate with his feet and roll you over or pull you into a closed guard.

Here's an example of the closed guard. By using a closed guard position, you can buy some time by pulling your opponent in close to you. Like they said in the gangster movie, "Keep your friends close and your enemies closer!" By keeping your opponent close to you, you limit his movement and give yourself time to decide what to do next or set him up for something you have in mind. Bill has pulled Ben on top of him and closed the space between his body and Ben's body. Bill has hooked his ankles together and is squeezing Ben's body with his legs. Bill also has wrapped his arms around Ben to close the space between their upper bodies as well. Bill could have pulled with his hands on Ben's head to pull it close to him, but he's done a good job of closing the space and buying some time (and control of Ben's body) until he decides what to do from here.

Here Mark is using his feet and legs to manipulate the top grappler, John. Grapplers who are good fighting from the guard use their feet and legs as if they are hands and arms. Manipulate your opponent, control the distance he is from you and set him up for a scoring move. Mark is pushing on John's hips in this photo, but he could be pushing on John's knee, chest, shoulder or any part of the body to manipulate and control him.

Mike is using a double grapevine to control Steve's legs and lower body. There are many guard positions and ways to use your body and appendages to manipulate your opponent.

Jake has jammed his right leg across Josh's belt line and is using his leg to keep Josh at a distance comfortable to him. In this situation, Jake is flat on his back and is pushing Josh away far enough so that he can get to his hip or buttocks to gain mobility to set Josh up for a rollover. This is another example of the many ways you can control your opponent if you are fighting from the guard position.

Stay South of the Border and Keep your Hand and Arm Movements Tight and Close

Steve is in Ronnie's guard, making sure to stay below Ronnie's belt (or hip) line and not rush in and extend his reach (and body) too far. Steve also makes sure to not reach out too far or hook under Ronnie's leg with his arm as Ronnie could quickly counter with a triangle from the bottom position.

The Importance of Shrimping

The "shrimp" is a fundamental skill in all grappling sports. Knowing how to curl up in a fetal position and place yourself in a better position or get out of a bad situation is important. This photo shows Josh starting his escape from a side hold by shrimping into Travis.

Shrimping Drill

Bryan is demonstrating a fundamental (and important) skill for grappling. I've always called this shrimping, but it may go by other names as well. Shrimping is the movement you will use to propel your body either away from or into your opponent to gain an advantage. Basically, you turn to one side and on one hip, curl up tightly, and push with your feet (usually both, but if necessary, only one) to propel your body in the direction you wish to go. I recommend that every grappler do some shrimping drills at every practice as part of his warm-up. It's a great addition to your warm-up and develops a fundamentally important grappling skill at the same time.

Bryan rolls to his left and draws his feet in tight to his body. His elbows touch his knees and he is in a fetal or curled position. Bryan's feet are pushing into the mat.

Bryan has pushed with his feet and straightened his legs, propelling him back. This action is useful to get away from an opponent if you are on your back and should be practiced every workout.

Blocking Your Opponent's Shrimp

Every move has a counter, or so it seems, and in this photo Nick (on top) is using his right knee to block Kirt from shrimping into him and start and escape. This is the fascination we all share with all forms of sport combat; the constant study and practice of skills and moves that work against each other or with each other. This is the "action-reaction-action" of grappling and wrestling that my friend Jim Schneweis often coaches to his wrestlers.

This photo shows how John is using his right arm to block Eric from shrimping in to start his escape. John has posted his right hand on the mat under Eric's right his and upper leg. This keeps Eric from curling his right leg and turning onto his right hip to start his escape.

Bear Hug Rollover (The Basic Rollover)

This is usually the first rollover I teach and shows new grapplers how to stay round and control the top man. As said earlier in this section, I have called these moves "rollovers" for many years, as have other people. They are now more commonly called "sweeps" and if you're comfortable calling these moves sweeps, it's certainly okay with me. It's my opinion that the word rollover describes the movement more accurately, but if you like calling these moves sweeps, keep using that term.

I've included this move to illustrate the point that you have to learn good basics before you can go on to more advanced or personalized moves from any position, and in this case, the guard. This rollover teaches a new grappler a lot more than simply this one rollover. You have to be comfortable fighting off your buttocks and getting a "feel" on how to establish yourself in this position. This also teaches a new guy how to coordinate his lower body and upper body together to control his opponent.

Mark, the bottom grappler, is sitting on his buttocks and has closed the space between his body and John's body by scooting his buttocks as close as possible to John's knees. In fact, if Mark is able, he should be almost sitting on John's knees. Mark is squeezing John with both of his legs and has pulled John in as close as possible to his body. Mark bearhugs John with both arms and basically locks the two bodies together as tightly as possible.

Mark starts to roll to his left side, firmly holding John in a bear hug. Mark wants to get as close to John as possible and stay round through the whole rollover.

Mark rolls to his left, staying as round as possible and rolling John with him.

Mark has rolled over on top of John.

Mark applies the vertical pin.

Cross Grip Elevator to Chest Hold

If you can cross-grip your opponent when you are fighting from the guard, you have an added advantage. Steve is using his left hand to grab low on Bret's left sleeve near the wrist and is using his right hand to control Bret's upper left arm. As he does this, Steve uses his left leg to jam between Bret's legs and wedge on the inside of Bret's right upper leg.

Steve has used his left hand to pull Bret's left arm across Steve's body and to Steve's left hip as shown. As he does this, Steve uses his right arm to further trap Bret's right shoulder and back. Steve has scooted his body away from Bret a bit for a bit more working room. Steve's left leg is jammed inside Bret's right upper leg.

Steve uses his right hand to pull Bret closer to him and reach over Bret's left shoulder to grab Bret's belt. As he does this, Steve continues to pull hard with his left hand in the cross-grip of Bret's left hand.

Steve starts to roll to his right and uses his right foot and leg to prop Bret's left hip and leg. Steve uses his right elbow effectively by driving down and in the direction he wants to roll Bret.

Steve uses his left leg to elevate Bret over as he uses his right leg in a whipping motion for more power and control of the action.

Steve has rolled Bret over and finishes with a chest hold.

Cross Leg Rollover to Chest Hold

Steve has Bret in his guard and uses both of his hands to grab Bret's left arm as shown.

Steve uses his left hand to grab Bret's left sleeve low at Bret's wrist and pulls Bret's left arm across Steve's body to Steve's left hip. As he does this, Steve uses his right knee and lower leg to jam across Bret's midsection at the hip or belt line. After doing this, Steve uses his right arm to reach over Bret's right shoulder and grab Bret's belt. Steve's left leg and foot are propped against Bret's right leg to help whip Bret over in the roll.

Another view of how Steve has jammed his right knee and shin across Bret's midsection at the belt line. Notice that Steve is "locking in place" Bret's left hip and upper leg with his right foot. Steve will now roll to his left hip and use his right leg to help roll Bret over.

Steve rolls Bret to Steve's right and Bret's left as shown.

Steve finishes with a chest hold.

Butterfly Rollover to Vertical Pin

Mark has John in his guard and has both of his feet wedged in John's hips as shown.

Mark has control of John's jacket for upper body control as shown. Mark uses both of his legs and feet to hook inside John's thighs immediately above John's knees.

Mark sprawls John out by pushing with his legs and this action pulls John down as shown. Mark uses his left hand to trap John's right arm.

Mark rolls John to Mark's left.

Notice how Mark has jammed his feet into John's thighs above John's knees.

Marks rolls over on top of John and finishes with the vertical pin.

Grapevine Rollover to Vertical Pin

Mike has Steve in his guard.

Mike uses both of his legs to grapevine Steve's legs and extend them as shown.

Mike quickly rolls Steve over onto his back

Mike finishes with a vertical pin. Mike could have been working a cross lapel choke on Steve and can use this rollover as a way to roll over on top of Steve and finish him with the choke as well.

Over Under Rollover to Vertical Pin

Mark has John in his guard and has used his left hand to reach over John's right shoulder and arm and grab John's belt. Mark uses his right arm to hook up and under John's left shoulder as shown. Mark is using his left foot as a prop at John's right knee.

Mark quickly rolls to his left and uses his legs in a whipping motion to make the rollover more effective.

Mark is rolling John onto his back and keeps good control with his arms on John's upper body.

Mark finishes with a vertical pin.

Double Leg Rollover to Double Trouble (Vertical Pin and Cross Lapel Choke)

Mike has Erik in his guard and jams his feet in Erik's hips. Mike's toes are pointed out with his heels inward. As he does this, Mike works in a cross choke on Erik's lapels. Mike makes it a point to scoot his buttocks in as far as possible toward Erik.

Erik stands up to start to pass Mike's guard. As Erik does this, Mike pulls in tightly on Erik's lapels and scoots his buttocks in between Erik's legs as far as possible.

Mike rolls back over his left shoulder in a rear somersault, pulling Erik over with him.

Mike rolls over on top of Erik into a vertical pin with the cross choke cinched in tight.

Saylor Shoulder Lock Rollover

My friend John Saylor used this rollover during his competitive judo career with good success. It starts with Eric being in John's guard. John uses his right arm to reach over Eric's right shoulder and grab Eric's belt as shown. John pulls Eric's head forward toward John's right hip.

This photo shows how John pulls Eric forward. Notice that John is using his right hand to grab Eric's belt and is using his right elbow to drive Eric's head down toward the mat and toward John's right hip.

John locks his hands together in a square grip and continues to drive Eric forward. John squeezes hard on Eric's upper body and shoulder and puts a lot of pressure on Eric's head and neck. This is a powerful shoulder lock.

John rolls to his left hip and buttocks as he uses his arms to pull Eric over with him. Notice that John is driving with his left elbow down to the left toward the mat. John is using his left leg to trap Eric's right leg and hip. This causes Eric to roll to John's left.

219

John has jammed his right foot inside Eric's left upper leg and is using his right leg to lift Eric as he rolls him. This is a variation of the basic elevator rollover.

John is rolling Eric to John's left side, all the while continuing to apply a lot of pressure on Eric's shoulder and neck. This pressure help make the rollover work much easier (for John anyway!).

John has rolled Eric over and is on top of him to apply the vertical pin or sit up into the mount.

Shrimp and Underhook Rollover to Vertical Pin

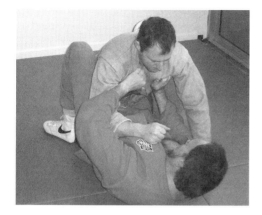

Steve is in the guard with Shawn between his legs.

Steve quickly rolls to his right hip in a shrimp position and uses his right hand and arm to hook under Shawn's left knee as shown. As he does this, Steve uses his right leg to start the rollover. Notice that Steve's head is very close to Shawn's left knee on the mat.

As Steve shrimps to his right, he uses his left hand to reach over Shawn's left upper arm and shoulder and grabs Shawn's belt to keep Shawn from posting with his left arm on the mat. Steve makes sure to post on the mat with his left foot for stability.

Steve rolls Shawn to Steve's left and Shawn's right. Notice that Steve has used his left foot and leg to trap Shawn's right leg and hip. Steve's right foot is pointed and driving hard.

Here is another view of the rollover.

Steve has rolled Shawn over and is on top of him.

Steve finishes with a vertical pin.

222

Knee Jam Rollover to the Straddle Pin

Jake has Josh in his guard.

Jake uses his right knee to jam into Josh's left ribs and uses his right shin to wedge under Josh's left inner thigh.

Jake jams his right knee and shin into Josh as he rolls slightly to his right hip.

Jake uses his left hand to reach over Josh's arm (to keep Josh from using his hand and arm to post onto the mat) and uses his left foot and leg to block Josh's left side.

Jake now shrimps hard to his right side and hip and as he does, he uses his right hand and arm to hook under Josh's right knee as shown. Notice that Jake still has his right knee jammed in Josh's ribs. Jake makes sure to keep his left foot planted on the mat for stability.

Jake pulls hard with his left hand on Josh's belt and scoops with his right hand and arm under Josh's left knee as shown. Jake starts to roll Josh to Jake's left.

Jake rolls Josh over onto his back.

Jake keeps his right knee jammed into Josh's ribs as he rolls over onto Josh, Jake drives his knee hard onto Josh's torso. Jake still is using his right hand to hook under Josh's left leg. Jake now uses his left hand to reach under Josh's neck for upper body control.

Jake uses his left foot and leg to post wide for stability as he pins Josh with the straddle pin.

Jake can uses his left hand to pull up on Josh's neck as shown to add more pressure to the hold.

Hip Whip Rollover

Andy has Jarrod in his guard.

Andy rolls to his left hip and uses his left hand to trap Jarrod's right wrist to Andy's left side at about the hip or low rib (or even to the mat). Andy uses his right hand to reach over Jarrod's right shoulder.

Andy continues to roll to his left side and turn his body to his left. As he does this, he puts his left leg close to the mat and will quickly whip his body to his left.

Andy uses his hips and right leg to whip hard into Jarrod as he uses his left foot to plant on the mat as shown. The explosive whipping action of Andy's lower body causes Jarrod to roll over.

Andy has rolled Jarrod over and finishes with a vertical pin.

Arm Wrap Hip Whip Rollover

Jarrod is attempting to use a bent armlock on Andy from the bottom. He can either really try for the armlock or use it as a set up on Andy to get the rollover. Jarrod is using a bent armlock from the bottom and has secured a figure 4 position with his arms on Andy's right arm.

Jarrod keeps control of Andy's right arm by lacing his right hand and arm and grabbing Andy's right wrist with his right hand. This isolates Andy's right arm. Jarrod has quickly rolled onto his left hip and is using his left hand to post out wide for stability.

Jarrod has used his left foot to plant onto the mat and is whipping his lower body (hips and right leg) hard into Andy. Jarrod still uses his left hand to post on the mat for stability and continues to lace his right arm around Andy's right arm.

Jarrod whips Andy over onto his back.

Jarrod finishes with a vertical hold or can sit up for the mount.

Ankle Trap Guard Pass

Steve is between Ronnie's legs in the guard and has grabbed the inside of Ronnie's knees as shown.

Steve uses his left hand and elbow to push down on Ronnie's right knee and leg.

Steve uses his left knee to trap and slide over Ronnie's right inner thigh as shown.

Steve places his left knee on the mat trapping Ronnie's right leg and as he does, Steve moves to his left over Ronnie's right leg. Notice how Steve is using his left foot inside Ronnie's right thigh above his knee to trap it.

Steve uses his right foot to trap Ronnie's right lower leg and ankle as shown as he continues to move to his left over Ronnie's right leg and hip.

This is a close view of how Steve has trapped Ronnie's upper leg and is using his right foot to trap Ronnie's lower right leg.

Steve quickly moves to his left and around Ronnie's side.

Steve uses his left arm to hook under Ronnie's neck trapping Ronnie's upper body. Steve does this in a deliberate manner and doesn't rush things.

Steve finishes with a side hold.

Nutcracker Guard Pass to Scarf Hold

Jon is between Travis's legs in the guard and uses his right hand to grab Travis's belt as shown. Make sure the right hand is palm up for more power and control. As Jon does this, he uses his right forearm and elbow to drive hard into Travis's crotch.

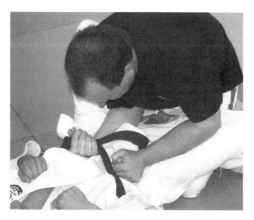

Jon stays compact and uses his elbows to push on the inside of Travis's thighs. This shows how Jon is controlling Travis with his right hand and arm.

Jon uses his left hand to push down on Travis's right knee and upper leg and makes sure to continue to press hard on Travis's crotch with his right arm.

Jon keeps firm control with his right hand and arm on Travis's belt and crotch as he uses his right knee to come across and move over the top of Travis's right thigh as shown.

Jon keeps his right knee and shin firmly on Travis's right upper leg as he quickly hops over Travis's right side (to Jon's left). Notice that Jon maintains firm control with his right hand and arm and hasn't let go of Travis's belt at all.

Jon quickly hops over Travis and has let go with his right hand and uses it to wrap around Travis's head for a pin. Notice how Jon has used his left leg to post wide for stability and support.

Jon finishes with a scarf hold.

Climb the Rope Guard Pass

Bret is on his feet with Mike on his buttocks in the guard. Bret uses both hands to grab low on Mike's pant leg near the ankle.

Bret uses his hands to trap Mike's lower legs together as shown.

Bret uses his left arm to wrap under Mike's ankles as he uses his left shoulder and head to help trap Mike's legs together.

Bret is now on his knees and low to Mike's lower legs, hugging Mike's ankles and lower legs with both hands trapping them.

Bret methodically works his way up Mike's legs making sure to keep tight control of Mike's legs and holding them together as shown. Bret makes sure to keep his head low and on Mike's legs.

Bret works his way up Mike's body and uses his left hand to hook under Mike's neck as shown. This helps control Mike's upper body.

Bret has worked his way up Mike's body and finishes with a chest hold.

Arm Trap Guard Pass

Steve is between Mike's legs in the guard. I like this move and was fortunate to use it a lot on opponents in this situation.

Steve uses his right hand to grab Mike's left sleeve low near his wrist. Steve uses his left hand to reach between Mike's legs and passes Mike's left wrist from Steve's right hand to his left hand.

Steve uses his left hand that has grabbed Mike's left sleeve low at the wrist and pulls Mike's left hand tight to Mike's left hip as shown.

Steve continues to keep Mike's left arm trapped as shown and uses his right hand to grab Mike's lower leg. As he does this, Steve starts to move to his left around Mike's left leg.

Steve continues to keep Mike's left arm trapped as he moves around Mike's leg. Steve stays low for better control.

Steve uses his right hand to push down on Mike's left upper leg and get past the leg as he does it.

Steve quickly moves to his right around Mike's body all the while keeping Mike's left arm trapped with his left hand

Steve finishes with a side hold and now lets go of Mike's left hand and uses his left hand to hook between Mike's left leg as shown to prevent Mike from shrimping into him.

SECTION FIVE:
Pin Switching

"The primary thing is not to let your opponent recover his position, even a little."

~ Miyamoto Musashi

What Pin Switching Is

When you apply a pin on an opponent, his natural instinct is to try to get away. Your natural instinct is to do your best to keep him there. In a good number of cases, you will have to switch from one pin to another to maintain control of his body and keep him from getting up. Whenever you move from one hold to another and maintain control of your opponent, you are "pin switching." Sometimes you will switch from a pin to an armlock or other submission technique or switch from a pin to a striking attack. The idea is to maintain control of your opponent, immobilize him and restrain him from moving and escaping from your control. The pins we use in judo, submission grappling, MMA, sambo and sport jujitsu are what Gene LeBell calls "time holds." Basically, the grappler holding his opponent to the mat is parking his man on his back for as long as possible until he takes the starch out of him or maneuvers the bottom man into a better position for a submission technique. Also remember, that if you don't have to switch from one pin to another, don't do it. Your goal is to restrain your opponent and immobilize him with him mostly on his back or backside. If you're holding so tight that he can't move, then all the better for you, but if you sense you're losing control of him, you will need to switch from your initial pin to another pin, or even to a submission technique.

It's a good idea to drill on pin switching on a regular basis. Make it a point to start with a specific pin, and then move to another, then on to another. Have your training partners offer varying levels of resistance from total cooperation (to develop good skill) to complete resistance. My friend John Saylor does a "round the world" pin switching drill where he starts from a specific pin (for instance, let's use the upper body pin) and switches to a series of pins in a complete 360 degree sequence around his partner, eventually ending back up in the upper body pin. Generally, though, you will switch from one pin to another, and maybe even a third pin, if necessary. In judo competition, it's not unusual to see an athlete switch from one pin to another to maintain control until the time runs out and the match is won. There are many ways to switch from one pin to another. This book will only show a few that I believe are fundamental for you to learn. It's a good idea to get with your training partner and experiment on pin switching in practice. See which work best for you and your style of grappling. Obviously, if you are a mixed martial arts fighter, you will want to develop moves based around your mount position. If you are a judo athlete, work on the pin switches that work best for your sport. Then if you are a sambo wrestler, definitely work on pin switches as well as switching from a pin to a submission technique after you've accumulated your points for the hold-down. Personalize, refine and drill on these moves so that they work for you when you need them.

When you switch from one pin to another, be economical in your movement. Generally, do things in increments and not in big, obvious moves. Move from point A to point B, then on to point C, and eventually point D. Be patient. Remember, you're on top and he's on the bottom. Since you're in a better position than he is, do everything you can to keep him there.

Upper body Pin to Rear Scarf Hold

This is a good example of what a pin switch should look like. John will move from one pin to another without losing control over his opponent Eric.

John starts out with an upper body pin. As Eric starts his escape and John senses that he can't maintain enough control to keep Eric down, John will start his pin switch.

John posts his right leg out to the side, which gives him room to sit through with his left leg as shown. John maintains good chest contact with Eric.

John and completed his sit through and snugs Eric in tightly for the hold.

Chest Hold to Vertical Hold (Sneak Knee Over)

Kirt is holding Erik with the chest hold.

Kirt uses his right knee to move up onto Erik's midsection and hip. Kirt keeps good control of Erik with his hands and arms and wants to change position without losing any control.

Kirt quickly moves over and switches to the vertical pin.

Chest Hold to Rear Scarf Hold to Vertical Pin
(Leg Kick Over)

Jarrod is pinning Chris with the chest hold.

Jarrod starts to sit through in the direction of Chris's feet. Jarrod uses his right leg to post to give himself room to sit through.

Jarrod sits through and into a rear scarf hold. He can stay here and maintain this hold if he wishes.

Jarrod chooses to switch over to the vertical pin and uses his right leg to swing over Chris. As he does this, Jarrod makes sure to use his right hand to scoop in on Chris's left hip and upper legs to move them together. Doing this makes it easier for Jarrod to swing his leg over.

Jarrod finishes with a vertical hold.

Rear Scarf Hold to Upper Body Hold

Nick is holding Kirt with a rear scarf hold.

Nick posts with his right leg and moves his knee up giving himself room to move his left leg backwards.

Nick settles in with an upper body pin.

Straddle Pin Series

This is an interesting and effective series that uses pinning skills and armlock skills. Jake is on his buttocks with Josh in his guard. Jake's buttocks are very close to Josh's knees.

Jake spins in for a cross-body armlock (juji gatame) shrimping to his right side and using his right hand to hook under Josh's left knee as shown. Jake isn't flat on his back, he's curled up and on his right hip and side. Jake's right leg is pushing against Josh's left ribcage.

Jake swings his left leg over Josh's head and neck, making sure to hook the head.

Jake rolls Josh over onto his back and can apply the cross-body armlock or use a straddle pin. Notice that Jake is using his left hand to hook under Josh's near (right) arm. Jake is using his right hand to continue hooking Josh's left leg.

Jake uses his right foot to draw up under Josh's far (left) shoulder and moves his left knee up under Josh's head as shown. Jake holds firmly with his hands and rides Josh with the straddle pin (uki gatame).

Here's another view of the straddle pin. Jake keeps his head low to keep his position a strong one.

Jake can switch to another variation of the straddle pin by leaning back as shown. Jake is using his right hand to post on the mat between Josh's legs. Jake has moved his hips down and lower on Josh as well. Basically, Jake is doing anything he can to stay balanced and continue to control Josh.

This variation of the straddle pin is a strong one. Jake is using his left hand to grab his right foot.

Josh has managed to roll away from Jake.

Seeing that he has lost control of the straddle pin, Jake swings his left leg over Josh's head. Notice that Jake keeps control with his left arm on Josh's near (right) arm.

Jake rolls back with a cross-body armlock and gets the tap out.

If Jake had chosen not to go for the cross-body armlock, he could have switch to the vertical pin. As Josh tried to roll away from Jake to escape the straddle pin, Jake uses his right hand to post on the mat as shown. Jake also shifts the weight of his body over onto Josh's midsection. Jake is also using his left hand to post on the mat near Josh's head for stability.

Jake moves over on top of Josh quickly.

Jake finishes with a vertical pin.

Scarf Hold to Triangle Pin

Bryan is holding Chas with a variation of the scarf hold.

If Chas uses his left arm to try to hook under Bryan's right leg in an effort to escape, Bryan will draw his right leg up closer to Chas as shown.

Bryan rolls over Chas as shown and posts with his right hand on the mat for stability. Bryan starts to kick over with his right leg as he stays on his left hip.

Bryan uses his right leg to hook over Chas's head. Bryan uses his right hand to grab Chas's wrist as shown. Bryan's weight is leaning forward over Chas's body.

Bryan rolls over onto his head and left shoulder and continues to pull on Chas's left wrist. Bryan forms a triangle with his legs as shown. Bryan can apply a choke or settle in for the pin.

SECTION SIX:
Pin Escapes

"It's embarrassing laying there on your back looking at the lights in the ceiling. I do everything I can to avoid it!"
~ *Kenney Brink, U.S. National Junior Champion in Judo and Sambo*

The best time to escape from a pin is the instant you have been put onto one. This is the split second before your opponent has cinched his hold in and restrained you to the mat. There's a very small window of opportunity there for you, so you must react quickly and attempt your escape. Another time for escape presents itself when you've been held for a while and you work, one small move by one small move, to free yourself.

Really, the best escape for a pin is not to get into one, but if you are put into a pin or hold, keep your cool and get to work. Let's face it; your odds of getting out of a pin are not always good. Be realistic and work hard on controlling the position, even if you do nothing but get out of trouble and get to a neutral situation. Also, face the fact that some pins are harder to escape from than others. It's been my experience that the chest hold is hard to escape from and this is why it's so popular and why I emphasize its use so much, but any pin that is applied tightly is effective. I recommend that you drill on pin escapes on a regular basis. At Welcome Mat we call this drill "lock ins." Basically, your partner locks you into a pin and you try to get out of it. Have your partner do his lock ins in varying degrees of cooperation from total cooperation to 100% effort in trying to keep you under control. This is also a good pin drill for the top grappler as he gets used to holding a resisting opponent to the mat, and it has the added benefit of toughening you up to a good degree. Honestly, I've been involved in the grappling sports since 1965 and one of the areas anyone, and I mean anyone, pays the least attention to is how to get out of a pin. Maybe it's because we're all optimists or maybe it's something we don't want to think about, but getting out of a pin is something nobody works on regularly. Everybody gets pinned during the course of his career, but if you can learn the skills necessary to avoid getting caught in a pin and then how to get out of one once you've been pinned, you will be a better athlete for it.

I recommend that you work on the shrimp escape from a side hold as your first pin escape to learn. Get good at shrimping, as this movement is vital to a good grappler being able to move freely and with mobility on the mat. I try to instill in my athletes the concept of immediately shrimping into the guy that pinned him and try to pull him into his guard or push him away. With this in mind, let's start the first pin escape.

Shrimp Escape from the Side Hold and Pull Him Into Your Guard

Travis is using a side hold on Josh. Josh starts to shrimp in and toward Travis and turns quickly onto his right hip. As he does this, Josh, used his right hand to jam in Travis's left hip and push hard on it. Josh can use his left hand to push against Travis's left shoulder as well.

This back view shows how Josh uses his feet to push against the mat as he shrimps into Travis.

Josh uses his right knee to jam into Travis's midsection as Josh continues to shrimp in.

Josh swings his buttocks over to his left, rolling onto his back and pulls Travis into his guard as shown.

Shrimp Escape and Counter with the Straddle Pin

Josh has Jake in the chest hold.

Jake shrimps into Josh and uses his right knee to jam into Josh's midsection.

As Jake shrimps into Josh, he uses his right hand to hook under Josh's left leg as shown. Jake also uses his left hand to grab Josh's jacket or belt as shown. Jake wants to jam his right knee across Josh's midsection.

Jake rolls Josh over as shown.

Jake uses his right knee jammed across Josh's midsection to help drive Josh over. Jake uses his right arm to scoop up and help lift Josh over as well. Jakes uses his left hand to pull Josh over using the jacket or belt.

Jake rolls Josh over and on top of him and finishes with the straddle pin.

Underhook and Rollover from the Mount

Chas is sitting on Chris in the mount position.

Chris uses his right hand to hook under Chas's left leg at the same time he shrimps to his right. Chris also is using his left hand to grab Chas's right sleeve near the triceps.

Chris uses his right hand to hook and scoop up and under Chas's left knee as shown as he uses his left hand to pull Chas over.

Chris rolls Chas over and on top of him as shown. Chris is out of trouble and now in a neutral position.

Bridge and Roll Escape from the Scarf Hold

Drew is holding Bryan with the scarf hold.

Bryan uses his left hand to reach around and grab onto his right hand as shown. As he does this, Bryan moves his body as close to Drew as possible. Notice that Bryan's feet are firmly on the mat with his knees up.

Bryan hugs Drew as hard as possible and jams his right hip as far as possible into Drew's body.

Bryan bridges and pulls Drew up directly over his head.

Bryan quickly rolls over and onto his left shoulder, rolling Drew with him. Don't make a common mistake of letting your feet slip out or not using both of them to drive onto the mat. Bryan is using his feet in this bridging action as his anchor and base.

Bryan has done the bridge and roll and rolls over on top of Drew.

Bridge and Roll Escape from the Chest Hold

Drew has Bryan in the chest hold.

Bryan grabs his right wrist with his left hand and hugs Drew very hard.

Bryan moves his body as close to Drew as possible making sure to keep his feet firmly planted on the mat for a base.

Bryan explodes into a bridge directly over his head pulling Drew with him.

Bryan quickly rolls over his shoulders and onto his left shoulder bringing Drew with him. Notice how Bryan is arching and driving against the mat with his feet as he rolls Drew over.

Bryan rolls Drew over and settles into a chest hold.

Wedge and Scoot Escape from the Scarf Hold

Drew has Bryan in the scarf hold.

Bryan uses his left forearm to jam up and under Drew's head at the ear. Bryan uses his right hand to grab his left wrist for more power. This action drives Drew's head up.

Bryan quickly turns his hips in toward Drew as shown.

Here's another view of how Bryan turns his hips in toward Drew as he wedges his left forearm under Drew's head and ear. Bryan now pulls his head down as well.

Bryan drives hard and rolls Drew over onto his back. Bryan sits up onto his right hip and has a strong base with his legs.

Here's another view of how Bryan has driven Drew over and Bryan is now on his right hip.

Bryan counters with a chest hold.

About The Author

Steve Scott holds advanced black belt rank in both Kodokan Judo and Shingitai Jujitsu and is a member of the U.S. Sombo Association's Hall of Fame. He first stepped onto a mat in 1965 as a 12-year-old boy and has been training, competing and coaching since that time. He is the head coach and founder of the Welcome Mat Judo, Jujitsu and Sambo Club in Kansas City, Missouri where he has coached hundreds of national and international champions and medal winners in judo, sambo, sport jujitsu and submission grappling. Steve served as a national coach for USA Judo, Inc., the national governing body for the sport of judo as well as the U.S. Sombo Association and the Amateur Athletic Union in the sport of sambo. He also served as the coach education program director for many years with USA Judo, Inc. He has personally coached 3 World Sambo Champions, several Pan American Games Champions and a member of the U.S. Olympic Team. He served as the national team coach and director of development for the under-21 national judo team and coached U.S. teams at several World Championships in both judo and sambo. He was the U.S. women's team head coach for the 1983 Pan American Games in Caracas, Venezuela where his team won 4 golds and 6 silvers and the team championship. He also coached numerous U.S. teams at many international judo and sambo events. Steve conducted numerous national training camps in judo at the U.S. Olympic Training Centers in Colorado Springs, Colorado, Marquette, Michigan and Lake Placid, New York. He also serves as a television commentator for a local MMA production and conducts submission grappling clinics for MMA fighters. As an athlete, he competed in judo and sambo, winning 2 gold medals and a bronze medal in the National AAU Sambo Championships, as well as several other medals in smaller national sambo events and has won numerous state and regional medals in that sport. He was a state and regional champion in judo and competed in numerous national championships as well. He has trained, competed and coached in North America, South America, Europe and Japan and has the opportunity to train with some of the top judo and sambo athletes and coaches in the world.

Steve is active in the Shingitai Jujitsu Association with his friend John Saylor (www.JohnSaylor-SJA.com) and has a strong Shingitai program at his Welcome Mat Judo, Jujitsu and Sambo Club. He has authored several other books published by Turtle Press including *ARMLOCK ENCYCLOPEDIA, GRAPPLER'S BOOK OF STRANGLES AND CHOKES, VITAL LEGLOCKS* and *CHAMPIONSHIP SAMBO*, as well as the DVD, *CHAMPIONSHIP SAMBO.* He has also authored *COACHING ON THE MAT, SECRETS OF THE CROSS-BODY ARMLOCK* (along with Bill West), *THE JUJI GATAME HANDBOOK* (along with Bill West), *PRINCIPLES OF SHINGITAI JUJITSU* (along with John Saylor) and *THE MARTIAL ARTS TERMINOLOGY HANDBOOK,* as well as the DVD, *SECRETS OF THE CROSS-BODY ARMLOCK.* Steve is also active in training law enforcement professionals with Law Enforcement and Security Trainers, Inc. (www.lesttrainers.com).

Steve is a graduate of the University of Missouri-Kansas City and teaches jujitsu, judo and sambo full-time as well as CPR and First-aid. For over thirty years, he worked as a community center director and coached judo, jujitsu and sambo in various community centers in the Kansas City area. He has conducted about 300 clinics and seminars across the United States and can be reached by e-mailing him at stevescottjudo@yahoo.com or going to www.WelcomeMatJudoClub.com. For many years, he was active as an athlete in the sport of Scottish Highland Games and was a national master's champion in that sport. He is married to Becky Scott, the first American woman to win a World Sambo Championship. Naturally, they met at a judo tournament in 1973 and have been together ever since.

Steve's first coach, Jerry Swett, told him as a teen-ager that he had a God-given gift for teaching and this impelled Steve to become a coach, and eventually, an author. Steve's second coach, Ken Regennitter, helped him start his judo club and loaned him the mat first mat ever used at the Welcome Mat Judo, Jujitsu and Sambo Club. Steve owes much to these kind men. His life's work and most satisfying accomplishment has been his effort as a coach to be a positive influence in the lives of many people.

Index

Symbols